Trilogy:
'He Heals the Broken Hearted'
Book 1

Treasures of Darkness:

Facing the Pain and Finding the Light

Marina Carrier

I will give you the treasures of darkness, and I shall open unseen secret things to you, so you may know I, the Lord God, who call you by your name, am the God of Israel. (Isaiah 45:3)

Dedication

To Father John Maitland Moir, who saw Who I lived for before I fully knew it myself.

And to Chris, my son, who taught me the nature of True Love, was given a vision of the Book Cover, and drew it for me to give to the designer.

Thank you to both these dear souls.

To request permission contact marinax7@btinternet.com

Acknowledgements

I thank all those who imaged a loving, caring God to me, even when my soul was so ignorant: the kindness of Mrs Davy when I was a child, and the headmaster at my first job, Mr Purvis. He encouraged my work for and with the pupils and gently taught me about protocols with authority without crushing my spirit.

Since being brought back to faith, and the Church, I thank **Holy Trinity Church, Nailsea** – in particular, **Rev John Simons** and all those who saw me through my infancy as a committed Christian. And Clay McClean whose Healing and teaching gave hope. And thanks to **St Francis RC Church** Nailsea, where **Fr Graham** gently taught confession, and God's enormous love for the broken-hearted.

I also want to thank **l'Abri** in Huemoz, Switzerland, and my tutor **Jim** and his wife, and all the community who opened up shut doors in my heart.

And **Pere Milan**, in Champery, who encouraged me with the work of the Holy Spirit. And in that parish, **Theresa** and **Bernadette**, who gave of their resources to a stranger in their midst. And to **Ann,** who made my 'exile' in St Gingolph, France a joy when I had to leave Switzerland.

And to Srs of St Clothilde in Switzerland in Aigle, and **Franklin** the refugee– and to **Susan Barter** (Nailsea) who drove to return me and my bike to England.

I realise how many people, like **Ineka and family in Kintyre,** when I was called to Scotland, have enriched my soul and, finally led me into the Orthodox Church. Thanks to my **God-Mother Helen** and all my brothers and sisters in Christ, at **St Andrews in Edinburgh**, and **The Nativity of the Mother of God in Walsall** and all the **Birmingham area parishes**.; not least **Maria-Julia** who set 'Finding Pearls in God's Care', to music.

And since 2007, the **Community of Sisters and Mothers at a Monastery** along with **FB**, and **L** his wife, and the Gerondissa of the Monastery who annually welcomes me, and always spiritually feeds me.

And to those who witnessed 'friendship' to me over many years, Christina and Friedrich who showed me what it meant to be loved humanly, now living in Vienna; Janet in Todmorden; and Jim and Carol – the latter 3 helping me on my faith journey; and Jay who not only prayed me into the Kingdom, but has stayed close in His Love for over 30 years.

And to new friends in Christ, both within and outside the structured church. Thank you Indira, for all you have taught me and enabled me to open up to receive the Love of God as free-gift of Salvation, that I may grow into the flower God intended.

And my book helpers: Brian and Chelsea, Tatiana for the Book-cover design, Carl my editor, B.Raphael, and Andrew, for their constant support to keep me moving forward on the path of Love.

To You all, THANK YOU.

Foreword

These are the spiritual memoirs of a soul who has never ceased to be hungry and thirsty for righteousness, a Christian who has been battling in the waves of the rough sea of this life with only one guiding star and destination: our Lord Jesus Christ.

I have known Marina Carrier for over twenty years and have come to appreciate the honesty of her heart, the frankness of her conduct and her uncompromising commitment to do God's will.

Everyone who walks on this path of obedience to the Truth will suffer the force of a strong opposite wind. And Marina has suffered this opposition a lot. This is why her writings are not the result of contemplation alone; they are also the fruits of prayer and experience forged in the furnace of trials which the Lord permits to come to those whom He loves.

As an Orthodox Christian Bishop I have a word of advice for the Orthodox reader: please, do not be bogged down by the question of the exactness of the spiritual language used by Dr Carrier; this is neither the point nor the strength of this book (in any case God relates to every one of us in a unique way). Rather, read it as the frank confession of a soul who would sacrifice all she has to keep the "pearl of great price" and who is humble enough to be willing to listen and be a disciple for the rest of her life.

Bishop Raphael of Ilion

Introduction

1993- Nailsea: A Prayer after Getting Lost on a Walk.

I had a map,
I planned the way
But no way could I find..

So too Lord in my life –
But I cannot plan
My peace and joy –
I cannot bring myself
To Your purposes for me.
So battling fear
At not knowing where I was
I gave my feet to the Spirit;
Why fear a loving God?
(and You led me home!)

"I am the Way, the Truth and the Life"
I am in Christ -
I **am** in Christ -
I am **in** Christ –
In Him I live and move and have my being.
Lord God in Your strength
Let me live this Truth.
Let my life proclaim
Your glory.
Lord do not rest,
Until my salvation in You
Shines from me.
Till my righteousness through You
Shines out like the dawn –
My salvation like a blazing torch.

The Lord always prepares us for what He is going to do and in 1994, as I was preparing to leave Nailsea, I wrote, "the Lord convicted me of my arrogance – my reluctance to go slowly, and metaphorically to drive in the slow lane, with those who go slowly…in other words, my real humility is about nil!' and then I added 'At my farewell last night at St Francis RC Church, Mick, when praying for me, felt that **all my ordered life would become disordered**.

'And as I worshipped, the Holy Spirit asked me what I wanted of Jesus, I replied,

'that I may be free to worship Him in love, and to love others in humility; to love the unlovable and lame and lost, like Peter (a lost soul in Nailsea I had been asked to pray for); and that I would be able to release to Him the desire to be loved.'

Deep in my heart
God speaks
Pulsing His love for me
Conducting the music of life,
Silently waiting
For me to listen.

'Child, as befits my bride,
You shall be adorned
In garments of praise
For your King;
Adorned in Light
Of Truth of the Word;

Lovingly borne
In the Arms of Mercy
Carrying My Light
To the world;
Holding out My Love
To those who have no hope,
To those lost in the darkness
And spiritual despair.

No longer will you be called
Despairing, hopeless and lost-
But you will be called
Joyful one,
Patient and calm,
Glorious light,
Overcoming one.

I will do this
Through the power
Of the Holy Spirit-
AS YOU SEEK MY WILL
AND YIELD TO MY LOVE,
MY SPIRIT AND MY LIFE.

"I shall reduce you to a naked rock and make you into a drying ground for fishing nets, never to be re-built, for I Yahweh have spoken – declares the Lord Yahweh" (Ezekiel 26:14)

Readers Invitation

June 2022- I write for you, dear Reader, as much as for me, because truly in Christ, we are all One. And those of you who have suffered, particularly as children, are particularly held in God's Heart though we may not be conscious of it.

Yet we are all children of God, made in His Image, and we have all lost closeness to our Truth, to the Father's Heart and our willingness to serve and love in humility. I loved the gifts God had given me, and didn't want my littleness, pain and dependence on the Father, so I lost integrity and the very Essence of my Being. This is why Jesus said that to follow Him, we need to 'take up our crosses', which means we need to recognise and own them because they hold the Secrets of Grace and Love, so we can also "become like little children" (Mark 10:15).

It is true that God the Father carried me (and maybe you) through childhood traumas, and provided a living through the Holy Spirit of Truth in the intellect, in Education. But purity of heart was hidden in the broken heart, along with Love. And He had to enable me to accept my brokenness to bring restoration. As was once spoken to me when I was unwilling to experience the pain, *'If you have a wound, even if the surface is healed, but inside it is unhealed, infected, and causing great damage; you have to go into hospital to get it exposed, purified and healed'.*

So pain has to be faced, but with the Great Healer in charge. And He doesn't make mistakes or make it impossible if we surrender our will daily – to His Will in His Love in humility.

And then we can grow again in mature relationships, able to hear the Truth within, and learn to live and love again without trying to control anyone. We have self-control through the Holy Spirit of Love in obedience to God the Father.

Richard Rohr*, writing about 'Responding instead of Reacting', makes this clear:

"I believe we are made for love, that our natural abiding place is love, and that we in fact *are* love. Our absolute foundation is

communion
with God and others. This is the 'deepest me' to which we must return before we act.

From this foundation, we know we *must* act, and we *are able* to act from a place of positive, loving energy. Unfortunately, when 'triggered' by strong emotions, it is very difficult to come from that deep place of 'yes'."

(* For more on this, see Richard Rohr, *Emotional Sobriety: Rewiring Our Programs for 'Happiness'* (Albuquerque, NM: Centre for Action and Contemplation, 2011).)

This is why we need to allow our Lord to BE the Lord of our life, rather than react from the wounds and experiences of our childhood or later in life.

What can you expect to read here in this book dear Reader?
Some narrative grounds you in the 'story so far'; and the way I get to the PLACE where God provides the right conditions. These include both my willing heart, and the specific circumstances, where it is easy to 'experience and face pain' but at the same time know the wonder of the path the Holy Spirit is enabling.

So you will also find what one reader called, 'A book of personal psalms,' –varied poetry which tell the pain, the crying out to God, and the awesome praise and gratitude for the redemption of His Love and Presence.

You will find narrative of the 'daily work' alongside the 'listening' and being obedient to the creative and healing tasks of God in that place.

You will experience the gradual shift as the pain is transformed to new life, hope and purpose.

I invite you, dear Reader, to join in this journey and make it your own – allowing yourself to be aware of any 'reactions' that emerge. Write for yourself what pain/wound is emerging and listen for God's Truth and healing. See * on next page.

Notes for Readers

All writing in ITALICS either denotes words discerned as coming from the Holy Trinity – (sometimes it was clear Who was speaking) – or Words from Scripture.

**NB* I have invited your personal facing of pain, triggering of pain, or 'wanting to run away' by leaving the R-hand side of the poetry pages blank for you to write on. Thus you can make this a stepping stone to your own journal of listening, and receiving God's mercy and grace, through your own Inner Being/Heart.

Table of Contents

1

Hope:

God Further Prepares the Ground of Faith.

Walsall April 2020 - Coronavirus Lockdown.

When I first came back to the church in 1990, called by God, and facing the exhaustion of the previous years working in higher education, I was told by the Spirit to start writing. I wrote what I was studying in the Bible; I kept a record of my first prayers and how they tied in with Scripture, and how they were answered; I kept journals of daily reflections and what the Spirit was prompting me to read; and copious notes of teaching from conferences and eventually talks from monks and nuns, cleansing me and showing me how to LOVE in Christ. And scattered in these journals was 'verse' – some of it clearly inspired while other examples were an attempt to find words for deep feeling or half-buried experiences.

And when I started to travel, I included more and more drawings (daily miracles themselves) of the wonder of what the Lord was showing me, which was His Love for me. So, from 1990 to 2020 I kept many notebooks, sketchbooks, and journals, some of them in French when I was living as a hermit in Switzerland. I wondered what God's purposes for them were. I needed the Holy Spirit to do the prompting and show me if, what and how?

Since being in Walsall, I had been living as a parish worker, and there has always been much work to do, so I ignored the promptings to set aside a day a week, at least, for simply retreating to my 'cell' and spending time alone with God. I was still afraid to go in the 'slow' lane, after nearly 30 years, but also subconsciously afraid of disapproval.

But since the lockdown, and self-isolating, I have been able to commit myself to more time in contemplation, studying and listening within. But still, no focus, until I found the journals of the time in Wales. A different sort of lock-down – but a foreshadowing of the depths that the Lord has plumbed since being here in Walsall. So, the re-writing started with what He had told me to leave in His hands in 1990 - re facing the depths of pain, dereliction – in being despised, rejected and traumatised ......yet alone with God!!!

So dear Reader, if you continue reading, be encouraged, that whatever trauma you have experienced, NOTHING is impossible for those who put their Hope and Trust in Christ. With Him, we do not need to run away from our pains or cover them up with substances, or even overwork. Nothing to cover the pain, except the Cross, Word and life in Christ, with constant trust in God the Father, in Faith, Hope and LOVE....**Yet in this journey, He brought me to the greatest sense of integration and One-ness in myself I had ever had.** As I describe more of my journey of faith into the pain within, travel with me, and allow the Lord to show you where you to need to pray, '*Lord I believe, help Thou my unbelief* (Mark 9:24).

All that is in the Dark will come to Light: -Setting the captives free:

I had moved to Kintyre in the West of Scotland in 1997, under the wing of Saint Columba, following signs given over the previous four years. My life became itinerant on the borders of Scotland and England in the East, and over on the West in Kintyre as I prayed for Scotland. I learned of the pain of Scotland through the battles with England in the past and continuing distrust of the English. My job was to intercede, to forgive, bless and to love. And I continued to make calendars in whatever area I was in, following the initial Holy Island Reflections Calendar I did while at Leith School of Art (Edinburgh) in 2000. I thus persevered with the gift of painting and gospel truth in what I was inspired to draw or paint. (Psalm 18/19: *v1 The heavens declare the glory of God; The firmament shows the creation of His hands.*')

I remained vigilant to people's needs, and because of Christ's work with me, had become involved in prayer for healing, both for and through me. Years later, 2010, I was at a bi-monthly Healing Prayer meeting in Edinburgh, with a friend. At the end of the meeting, I was prompted to ask the co-leader of the Meeting, a woman, to pray for me. Everyone else had gone apart from the priest, and she took me aside and prayed silently. She looked at me with great compassion and said, 'Oh my dear, what a great well of pain.'

It was some comfort to me that God knew the pain I carried. But I had promised Jesus when I first came back into the church that I would persevere in doing His work and allow Him to bring about the healing I needed, in His time and His way. I, therefore, accepted events as they unfolded and trusted in His grace to give me the strength and courage to persevere to do what He was asking of me.

Indeed, I could say this book is not so much about me but how the Spirit of God gives us great grace to 'Stand' and serve in His Name, while we are carrying our crosses and burdens. He gives us Grace throughout, and we need to trust in His timing and way. Hope and Love become the keys to our Peace. And when God chooses and provides, He lets us receive His gift of ongoing deeper purification.

If you lose your life, you will find it: (Disorder reigns!!)
While living in Campbeltown, Kintyre, I got to know three Roman Catholic hermits, who had left one of the Hebridean islands after trying and failing to set up a monastery. When my house was blessed by my Orthodox Spiritual Father, they were present and blessed by him to keep in touch with me. Subsequently, they were inspired to give the church they had left, to me, for the Orthodox Church. It had been received by a welcoming Metropolitan with a view to making a monastery. As I was part of the vision of the monastery, I moved to be on the Island, to stay in a caravan, in May of 2011.

I spent my days at the church praying Matins, the Jesus prayer, and Vespers, painting icons and producing 'Words of Life' which were left out for visitors to take. (These were quotes from the Bible on individual cards providing Words of Life on the themes of Hope, Love, Trust, Faith, and Peace.)

One of my joys was welcoming the many visitors who found the church (built atop ancient foundations tracing back to St Columba and Iona) in the middle of nowhere. Many of them came to find the graves of ancestors who had to leave the island during the clearances. Apart from the joy of serving and being in the church and being alive to the work of the Father in bringing people to the church, I was in a difficult situation re: the making of the monastery.

I finally had to face the difficulties of my position when I went to the Monastery (an Orthodox monastery for women) for the Old Calendar Christmas of 2012. Through the prayers of Saint Seraphim, I was able to acknowledge my pain and sense of loss and spoke to the Gerondissa* just before I left. She told me I should get out because it was not doing me any good, but she affirmed God's view of me as a nun. (*the Abbess)

But needless to say, she did not/could not tell me what I had to do instead. I spent the next five months on the island, or in Edinburgh staying with other people from the church of Saint Andrews, or in my house in Kintyre getting it ready to sell and seeking what I should be doing.

During this time, I contacted an old Spiritual Father who told me he had been praying for me and seemed to hear that I should look to Iona. Consequently, I followed up on every invitation to work on, or join, any retreats or pilgrimages that were going to Iona. The final one in August led me to stay in my caravan at the Village Hall of Fionnaphort, Mull, sharing the role of cook with another pilgrim, for one of Bishop Kallistos's pilgrimages to Iona.

I shared my position with some participants, and one of them told me of his small cottage that was nearly ready to rent out in Llanybydder, mid-Wales. I accepted his offer and moved my things down to this tiny one-up one-down cottage in September with a great sense of dread.

Only through another retreat to the Monastery in October was I freed of my fears. Two years before, while still in Kintyre, I had found myself in the Spirit, being invited to spend time with St Theophan as a recluse and write. But I knew not what this meant, so I had unknowingly led myself into difficulties, when I moved to the island, to the 'monastery'. However, Fr J, the priest I confessed to at the Monastery, spoke to me of 'going like St Theophan' as a recluse. He had no human knowledge of my previous calling, and so I accepted to move to Wales under the wing of Saint Theophan, knowing peace in my heart that God was with me. The house sale was completed the day after I got back from the Monastery and the day before I finally moved to Wales!

I was also comforted by a text from a Nun of the Monastery, who had recently had an operation. I texted her to say how happy I was she had been able to have her pain removed. I added – "I wish that I too could have my pain removed". She texted back very briefly: "I believe that **the way of the pain is the way of love**." These two affirmations of my pain and this provision of what came to be blessed as a Hermitage made the following work possible.
And you too, dear Reader, if you are reading this, may you be guided

by your love for Christ, and your desire to Love God with ALL you are, and to love your neighbour as yourself. While there are parts of ourselves we do not love, we cannot love others without judgement, and we have to be very aware of the understanding of God that we have. I had been blessed when I first came back to a 'church' faith, that I had learned to listen and use my intuition and be fed by the Holy Spirit and the Word of God. God had told me He wanted the Truth from me…not putting on a 'face' to cover up if I was feeling miserable, angry etc. I must say so…then He could help. This was the Hope and Trust I clung to as I had journeyed through the previous years, and now as I went into this tiny hermitage in Wales. Come with me…..

Dear Reader: Allow yourself to 'bathe' in God's Love in what you are reading – through an open and willing heart….without getting overwhelmed by anything that triggers your own pain, or that causes any other form of stress or confusion. **This will be practice for you as you continue with your life of faith.** As you sense any 'block or distress' be aware, and own it, but keep your focus on the Cross and simply put it there in faith - I invite you to practice living in the Spirit of Faith, Hope and Trust'.

2

Hope

Into the Wilderness with Listening Time in Trust

'The way of the Pain is the Way of Love'.

3 Fisherman's Cottages: Llanybydder- *

I committed myself to this tiny one up/one down cottage finally on October 28th 2012, having brought belongings from the Island church, and Kintyre-house at the end of September. *Having been a cow byre, it was very small, and I needed a shed (ordered immediately), in order to have iconography space.

Also, I discovered that the landlord had booked himself onto an Orthodox Study Course in Walsall which met on the 2nd Saturday of each month. I agreed to go with him as I could stay on the Saturday night with my sister in Penarth, ready for church in Swansea on the Sunday.

The priest-monk who had guided my path with prayer agreed to come and bless the little cottage but meanwhile, I lived a prayer rule which included early morning time dedicated to reading and seeking to be fed by St Theophan, and in silent listening and writing from the pain of my heart. I then 'got up' to do Matins and start the day.

I started writing on the eleventh of the eleventh, 2012.

Go in and find rest

So many years ago *
I held Your hand
thinking you would lead me
into the Light
out of The Cave .

But You led me in,
to face demons ,
memories,
lost hopes, dreams,
false gods and Christ's truth.

We walked together,
You and I
as one,
sometimes You,
or rebellious I.

And God used the journey,
20 years in time, praying,
serving, creating,
loving - each act
of Grace, redeeming.

And light shone
out of every loss,
disappointment
abandonment;
apparent dross.

And I grew deeper in debt
To you my God and Lord,
Saviour and Redeemer
And more dependent
And pure of heart.

And now death -
Impasse it seems -
My mind broken open
Facing disappointment
As a woman in the church.

But with you my Lord
St Theophan rejects
The world in obedience
To your Spirit.
Come Lord Jesus!

In the silence
Words knock at the door -
No noblesse-oblige
To do the work,
But Grace to listen.

So permission is given
At the gates of hell
For holy seeds
To find their fill
And bring the dark to light.

*In 1992 on retreat at a Priory in Oxfordshire.

**Saint Theophan felt called to retreat from the world, Amen.

Later that same morning:

No fire

No fire burns within
save a flickering wick of Hope*
and You've promised
a smouldering wick
You will not put out.

No worldly fire draws me
for more than a glance
as I descend
into hell in this death -
I see the barren landscape

of a broken contrite heart.
Here I battled with the sniper
who shot down all
signs of life and hope
for fear of retribution.

But now only silence,
From so many years ago,
And death reigns in the pain.
Come Holy Spirit of Truth
nothing separates me from Your Truth
and Jesus You descend with me .

HOPE *- Blessed are those that mourn - yet
my God , my God- why did you abandon me?
If I can just touch your cloak
I will be healed
and all will be well.

Holy Lord, I forgive, help Thou
my unforgiveness.

Immediate Reflection following the above: As I wrote the above darkness, and owned it -the love of God lead my spirit and opened doors in my heart and Spirit and in 'forgiving', -these were not simply 'words' but Spiritual realities being built in my heart -thus 'life' came out of 'death' in my heart/Inner being.' Glory to God. (*Hope is faith in things unseen.)

Forgiving

In forgiving, I am forgiven
and in the confusion of lovelessness
hope builds on faith
love builds on mercy
and a Star is created
to lead and guide.

And even in this darkness
The star shines
Bringing Light and Life into the dark.
And making a way in the desert -
Your will be done my God -
So simple and so pure -Amen

12th November 2012.

05:15

Forgotten

No will for good
In this death,
Weariness in striving
to do good,
prayer a burden
in its heaviness -

Holy Father
where are You?
Protect me from
the rain and rising river,
my false gods.
Have mercy on the lost.
Come Holy Spirit
come Lord Jesus..

08:41

Yet I will praise You

The star that promises to lead
lifts my heart and mind
to Truths that transcend
the rain, my broken heart,
and earthly suffering -
And gives me Hope
to choose to praise-
gives me grace to
read the words of those
who have trodden the path before -
so Theophan shines
a light of the Way;
And my soul and mind
Are strengthened to
choose for Christ
and follow His Path
Of trust and obedience
In the Father, through
The Holy Spirit -
loving the Father in
Trust, praise and
Perseverance.

To whom shall we go?
You have the Words of Eternal Life.

08:45

Beyond Obedience-The Cross of Christ. (Prompted* through the Holy Spirit)

Obedience, listening.
Yes.
Heart, mind and will
purified by grace -
given over to sin
and death on a cross
For the sake of Love.

Beyond knowing,
outside reasoning
suffering loss and sin
for Love's sake.

Interceding for the lost,
Compassionate for the broken,
Purified by grace
Purified by loss
No shame
No blame
In Love.
Father forgive them
They know not what they do.

*
I use the term 'Prompted' to indicate a movement in my heart/inner being which sometimes is a direct indication that I must write something, or be still, etc – but it indicates Spiritual guidance – usually by Father, Son or Holy Spirit.

Emptied

Solus -death on a cross
Abandoned by all but the women
and John,
all worldly joys, people, plans
left for others.

Yet I will praise you.
Oh death where is your sting
or grave your victory?
Come Lord Jesus
come Holy Spirit -
Lead kindly light.

09:11

Need

Deep in this death
Lies a spoiled child
Longing for Grace
Truth, justice and love.

She cannot hear or see
only touch and move. **(see below)

Lord Jesus Christ
Who saved by the cross
Who brings all together
In your prayer, have mercy on me …
That I may be healed
Of this loss, purified
From false gods and needs,
And provided for in
Purity of heart, and
Prayer for unborn *
Children and their mothers.

**It was some years later (2019) while at the Monastery, I was led to recognise the ongoing wound, of my mother's desire and attempt to abort me in utero because I was illegitimate, when of course I could not see or hear. I was led here in 2012 to a recognition of that wound but without understanding of anything but the deep pain I had.

* I marvel always when I 'see' evidence of the Holy Spirit of Truth at work when consciously 'we know not what we do'!!

22:40

Lost

Abandoned at birth
Lost in the world
without love -
No one committed
To my welfare
Save You my God.

Though the mountains
Fall into the sea *
Yet I will trust in You
Yet I will praise You - Amen
*(from Psalm 46:1-3)

A New Day....**13th November 2012**

06:30

(Turning to God to ASK)
Need 2

Many years ago my God
You told me I could not
Supply my need
As I sought to rest through
Holidays, and running away.
Yet you have provided
In many ways as I have sought You.

Now Beloved
In You is joy and peace,
Hope and resurrection,
Wisdom and love!
Why am I here
in this place of dereliction* ?

Forgive, forgive your mother
for her lovelessness, self-hatred
and joylessness. Forgive her,
forgive her intransigence,
silence, hatred of men.
Forgive her. Come Lord Jesus.

Mourning, a lost childhood,
mourning a lost soul,
mourning for love of God
that you may be comforted
that you may be strengthened
given heart, hope, vision. *Amen*
"Sacrificial lamb, I love you."

Facing realities....

*Although I had originally ordered a phone installation through Talk Talk, while still in Scotland, the reality was that only BT could supply the area – and in fact, with missed appointments, at least one because the cottages were hidden away off Station Road – I didn't get a phone line till nearly Christmas. The connection with the mobile could only be had through Orange and was intermittent to say the least! It challenged me greatly – but I must honour the work of the Holy Spirit- when it was crucial for me to give or receive calls or texts, I was given a connection in the cottage – otherwise, even for 'business' calls, I would need to go and patrol the car park on Station Road to find a signal - frequently under an umbrella!

Truth

In Christ is neither East nor West,
In Christ is the fullness
of human life, dependent on God,

Fully relating to others,
Dependant on no one
Knowing that God will provide
Because He promises.

07:15 (Revelation from God)

No Heart Beat

Your life stopped
When he raped
And silenced you -
- *left you, half dead -*
and no one came.
A body lifeless and will-less.
Forgiven by God and you
but no will to live or give –
except in obedience to God.
No heart, no life, no love.

(I drew this once -
a heavy weight stopping
the wheel from turning,
Or the balloon from rising.
The sniper shooting down life.
Dear Lord forgive me.)

Child, beloved daughter,
give me your hand
And I will wed you
to My purposes to uphold
and provide for you.
And I will make you
a Fisher of men.

Jabez

Born and raised in pain,
To the greater glory of God,
Serving, giving in righteousness -
Obedient to a loving Father
Who provided in truth
And protected. Glory to God.

But on the cross of dereliction
Jabez cries out,* "Help me,
bless me my God, that I may
Be free of further pain - yet
be obedient to your voice and plan".
Have mercy on your children.
**1 Chronicles 4:9-10*

08:34

Spirit

I read St Theophan
In relation to the Spirit
And I see what You gave
me through the years -
how Your Spirit lifted
My life by Your grace
My Beloved -
Now, together, we claim
This body for higher ground
In Love and unity
With soul and spirit.
Surrendered and
Bound in love
To Your Heart and Mind and Will
In Christ, the holy one of God.
Come Holy Spirit of unity.

8.40am

Darling of My Heart,
Beloved of my soul
dearest treasure of my Kingdom
give me your heart -
now!
I did - I do
Oh my Father God -
forgive me for my
self protection.
I desire, I am willing,
to be free in You -
without the sniper
shooting every thought.

Let me be willing to
take every thought
captive – a prisoner,
or sent packing -
Your Will be done.

Crucified for loves sake,
beyond knowing or human reason:
Beyond repentance or love
into the realms of Life
Darling --paint today -in My life
this is My Will for you. Amen
Glory to you my God Thank You.

(At the end of the day:) 'I needed to do admin work re the insurance but linked the need to find a phone connection, with taking the dog a walk. I then went into the studio /shed and worked till 3pm on setting up the space for painting, reading more of Aidan Hart's book on icon painting, and continued with corrections of the large Platyterra icon I had started on the Island. Glory to God.'

22:59

Love

Gentleness overcomes passion
Forgiveness overcomes striving
Graciousness overcomes sloth
Sleep brings rest for the weary
God bless and keep you.
Amen .

3

Overcoming Intransigence:

Accepting Pain and Loss of the Cross, in Love

4th November 2012

I woke early in the Spirit without the morning feeling of dread, and called on Jesus. Immediately consolation was in my heart. The words of the hymn "on the solid rock I stand, all other ground is sinking sand", came in my mind and suddenly I saw the truth of this because literally, we sink when we don't stand in Christ. So when I re-woke with the alarm at 6:00 AM, I was at peace and in Peace. Glory to God.

'My heart and my flesh fail
Oh God of my heart;
and God is my portion forever." (Ps 72:26)

06.40

Lies

They tell me I am lost,
broken, unrepentant,
wilful, neglectful ,
without love.
That I have no right
to stand in Christ
and seek to serve
For righteousness' sake.
Because I have this body.
Oh my Beloved
have mercy on me.

I have sought, knocked,
asked in faith and trust,
overcoming sin with You,
through You, You are God.
You gave me Your heart
to love and serve where
there was no love or will.
Beloved I give all I am
into Your hands.
This is Truth. You are Truth .
And You overcome lies
By Your forgiveness.

Father forgive them they know not what they do.

06.59

Lies II

The accuser calls me a liar
for wanting you my Lord,
pulls me to defeat
because of my unworthiness
because of my desire for rest
And comfort.
I have feet of clay
Beloved one -
but in You is hope - truth -
Life everlasting.
And I choose for You.

Have mercy on me
In my unworthiness -
Forgive me my lack of love
And build me in courage
That I may overcome
In purity of heart and gentleness
The frailty of this body,
The divisions of soul and spirit
And the lovelessness of my life.
Come Lord Jesus, holy one of God.

Gentleness. '*He shall come down like rain upon a fleece and as drops falling upon the earth.*' (Ps.71: 6)

The Spirit descends
Flows, upholds,
Uplifts, enfolds,
Purifying, bleeding,
Cauterising; feeling –
Even in the dark
The way of the Cross
To bring new Life.
Delivering life
From death.
Glory to God.

Your Will be Done

Not by might,
Not by power
but by My Spirit
Says the Lord .

Great mystery of Life,
Awesome Giver of Love
Come and abide in us
And all I pray for-
Father, Your Kingdom Come.
Amen

The Garden

Prayer
Praise
Surrender to Your Will,
Life, and love.
Overcoming death. Amen
(This was almost a rebuke by God – He was gently telling me His Ways would give me LIFE – I would not get life by not staying in bed and resting!!)

18:20

Loss

Confidence fizzled like a damp squib
And I walked the way of the cross
with no strength for any other.
I did what the world was asking -
BT phone calls, new house insurance,
getting online so I could get course details,
and my desiring wanted food.
The sense of loss of You
Too much for me to bear.
Have mercy on me a Sinner.

18.23

Though Nothing Grow in the Fields

The star **is** there
when I raise my eyes
and like Habakkuk*
I still proclaim
That You are
The God of my Salvation
And I will praise You.

Oh my God confirm
Your voice, heart,
Mind, will for me.
Father forgive them / me
They know not what they do.
Yet I will trust and praise you my God

*Habakkuk is a minor prophet but is well known for claiming that even though nothing grows in the fields and there are no cattle or sheep still He will trust in God, the God of His salvation.'

15th November 2012

(The alarm was normally set for 6.00am…but no specific time is put for the following:)

"Just read a little more of St Theophan re: 'Life in the Spirit'. Glory to God.

To the Spirit belongs:
1. Mind ….Fear of God.
2. Conscience – which depends on the will.
3. Prayer, which depends on feelings – Thirst for God.

and he reflects on the Spirit's love of beauty. How true this is – how difficult it is to see beauty in this place with so much clutter and no visible beauty outside.*. Oh Lord have mercy.

(*There are three 'cottages', all ex-cow byres, in a row, with gardens about 4 feet from front door to the path that passes in front of them and to one other beyond. My 'garden' is all pebbles. The other side of the path, is one of the walls of the extension to the shop on the main road. From the outside it is an unadulterated breeze block built building about 12 feet high. From the upstairs window I can see over the roof to trees by the river!!)

06.46

Expressing the inexpressible

Hope bursts like a flower
Scenting all around with fragrance,
Lighting the darkness with beauty;
Joy timidly peers out through sorrow
To shine His life:
Peace knows no bounds
In trust in the Living God,
Prayer combines, unites, radiates
All to the wonder of His love.

06:57

One word

United
In Christ
Faith
Hope
love
but the greatest of these
is Love .

Love
died
On
The
Cross,
Darling
Of
My
Heart
Save Me.

TASK: Create a home of Beauty

Pure and holy
Loving and true.
Gently
Without shame
With grace and trust.
'We' will do it TODAY .

07:04

Mercy

All for Christ -
Stark yet radiant
Pure in function
Coherent in purpose
Glory to God .

07:59

Out of the depths

Deep within
Lies waiting
A well of unspoken words
Bound to the mind and will of God.
Unbidden, they wait
For time and place to be ready
And the thirst to overwhelm. Amen

PS re 15th (a reflection at the end of the day on the Practical outworking of the Spirit in creating order and beauty in the 'cow-byre cottage!)

'I did get Beauty's (the Vizla-Collie-cross dog) jacket, and curtains for downstairs, finished and curtains ironed before H came at lunchtime to go to his father's. By God's grace, he realised it wasn't raining, it was Thursday and he could go to the field to get the washing machine! We went together, glory to God. So by night curtains were up, the washing machine was in the cottage (though it needs new washers) and some order restored.

Come Holy Spirit '

16th November 2012

07.00

Let Go

Heavenly Father – You are God-
I worship You, bow my knee to You
Alleluia - Alleluia - Alleluia -
To You alone be glory.

I thank you for this new day
For the rest of sleep
For the mystery of Beauty
Who sometimes acts like an angel.

I worship You my God,
That at the Name of Jesus,
My Spirit is lifted to Love.

Holy, Holy, Holy Lord
Thank You for Your provision
Yesterday, for grace, strength
And material provision for living.

I bind my heart, and mind
And will to Your Will
And trust in Your love
To uphold me……

Trust darling daughter in MY Love,
For you, for Mary. Pray at all times*
And do not let despair
Nor the weight of the task
Defeat you.
This is the day that the Lord
has made, Rejoice and be glad.

(*I am going to Mary, met through my landlord, to help her clear out her rubbish.)

07.20

Justice

Darling daughter
You have accepted the Cross
Without denying Me –
Let Me provide
For your needs.
Yes- rest in Me
To design and paint.

Let me make you
A fisher of men
Without comprehension-
Without compassion.*

I will lift you
To new heights
Above worldly desires
Above the sins of the fathers.
Above a sense of loss.

* I believe what the Spirit was saying was that I would not have conscious 'feelings', but God the Holy Spirit would bring this about.

07.50

The Surgeon

By the Light of the Holy Spirit
With the sword of the word of God
The wounds of soul are exposed
And cut out, and the Truth
Sets free the prisoner,
Gives adoption to the orphan,
Provide sight to the blind,
And hope for the despairing,
Till standing on and in
The Blessed Rock, no winds
Can rock the soul
Alive in Christ.

Purity

Oh blessed Lord, Holy Spirit
Truly by your light I see
The Impurity of my thought
Yet as soon as I acknowledge it
And confess my sin
It has gone under the surgeon's
Knife - at the name of Jesus,
Every knee shall bow.
Amen, Amen, Amen.

17th November 2012

07.21

The Morning

I wake with the new day
And look to You my Lord and God:
I praise You, love You, hope in You
And trust in Your divine grace,
To carry me in Your purposes
Despite this weariness
That envelops me like a cloud.
But in faith I embrace the weariness
To Your Heart, in your gentleness.

(I slept more - went to get dowel for curtain rails, finally got to Saint Peter's in Lampeter, just in time for a coffee and mince pies - Lord forgive – I felt alive in talking to the priest, who trained with someone I knew well from Nailsea, where I started back within a church. There was unity in Spirit in Christ.)

Comment
I feel I am given these 'external forays' as a balance to the internal work, 'a bruised reed I will not break'. I am reminded of St Sophrony who used to say when he was an Igumen at a Monastery in Essex:

'When standing on the edge of an abyss gets too much, stand back and go and have a cup of tea'. It seemed that this is what God provided for me too.

And for you too Reader. Stand back and rejoice in His Love for you – and have a cup of tea.

18th November 2012

I am in I AM – upheld – beheld-
Great mystery of Love Divine
Who hung on a Cross
To save our souls –
Lord Jesus, Your will be done
I trust in You. Father forgive them
They know not what they do.

Will-less* (see next page)

The world tells me to 'go for it',
My flesh tells me 'I need it' - but
My heart yearns to be with You -
Held and nurtured by a loving Holy Father
Sent and pure, wholly and true.
And my spirit defines the next task.

Dear Lord Jesus, Holy Spirit
My will is for You -
And I will praise You
But give me a governing Spirit
My God that I can choose
Each moment a Holy path.

Greek practice, reading the prophets,
Praying matins, the Kathisma
The Jesus prayer -
Printing a calendar for Margaret.
All demanding Your grace -
Attention to detail.

I cannot do these things my God
Without Your love, grace, truth
In me, through me.
Deliver me from all self-interest Lord.
Come Holy Spirit, purify me
Beloved Saviour, give me grace-

To overcome my half-heartedness
In wanting to be loved and cherished.
Provide my Beloved for SS today
And let the dominating desire
Be for walking a holy way
At one with You in Your Father's heart.
Amen

*Some years after this while at the Monastery, the Gerondissa suddenly declared to me that she believed that the gift that God had given me was 'poverty of spirit'. I began to see how true this was, and also how hard it was to live with when in the world. The more I surrendered to Christ, the poorer 'I' became – since truly Christ only did what He saw the Father doing, or what the Father told Him to do. Truly my life was hidden in Christ in God. I did not understand this 'gift' at this time of writing.

19th November 2012

22:40

Silent Sorrow*Upheld in Life

Silent as the grave
I praised You in my heart
Yet not I but your Spirit
Praised and gave me strength
Like those holding the arms of Moses.
And when I stopped praising
I fell and the enemy threatened.
Upholding and blessing,
Your Spirit held me
Through the day of doubt and sorrow*.
Yet I will trust you
And hope in You
Who redeems our life
from the pit.
Jesus uphold me
And overcome the darkness
And despair and defeat.
Lord have mercy.
Amen Beloved.
(Trust Me darling of my heart, I love you).

*There is nothing in the 'journal' to indicate the source of this disquiet. But in my ordinary diary there is a note that says: 'BT - further delay - engineers say external work allocated for Wednesday the 21st! Then BT will get in touch on Thursday.'

All the isolation and difficulty of communication challenged my trust in God, and truly only praise is the answer in these circumstances.

21st November 2012

06.25

Sorrow and Joy

Sorrow for sin
Joy in redemption;
Words that bear truth
My life hidden in Him
Who gave all for me-
And the world.
So I will praise
and rejoice that
Today I celebrate
With the Angels
In the feast
of the Entry of the Theotokos
into the Temple.
My Beloved
I have no goodness,
Bravery, purpose
Except in You
Have mercy on me. Amen
Receive me today.

24th November 2012

Joyless

Oh Beloved
I see not feel how beautiful You are.
I see the grace and strength,
Forbearance and love
You gave me yesterday
To buy the wood and materials
To make the shelving.
And one bookcase completed;
The other half ready
To be completed today.

Glory to You.
Forgive me
That I seek You
To rest in Your Heart
To be blessed by You
For today.

(Deeper) Forgiveness

How long oh Lord
How long?
You ask me to forgive her -
What depths my Lord
We inhabit to know
The pain and loss of an unloved,
Unwanted child.

Oh dear God have mercy.
But I sense in this
Situation now
I must continue to forgive
And bless those who rejected-
Father forgive them.

Unloved, Uncherished

Forgive me my God
I do not understand
The difference between
Loving and indulging?
What does it mean?
I give my body its needs-
Sometimes.
I succumb to a passion
For comfort – sometimes;
I ignore its needs when
It seems I must persevere
For Your sake.
Lord have mercy.

And in this cold
Your angels have held me
To do the work
I need to do.

So I stand against
The lie that I am unloved
And uncherished;
And trust in Your provision.
Come Lord Jesus,
I believe, help Thou my unbelief.

27th November 2012

Determined

My body lacks lustre
As it fights infection,
Mirroring my spirit
That fights temptations,
Distractions and desires.

Beloved I come to You,
Determined for You,
Body, Mind and Will
Given to receive
And to give for You.

I surrender the tasks
As a gift offering of love
That we may unite
In surrendering all to the Father-
The outcome in His hands
Through the Holy Spirit.

And the work for the Course*
O my Beloved-
I surrender my intransigence
To You.-
"Celebrate the prophets
My child, My daughter,
I will guide you.
Rejoice in My care
And provision.
Give this afternoon
To this work.
You are Mine.

*This course work was for the Orthodox Studies Certificate Course I was studying at Walsall each month.

Silence

Like a wall
Silence embraces
The Cross
Deep within.
I cannot hide
Nor overcome
But wait in Christ,
Determined
Not to run away.
God is my Hope,
Salvation
And Truth.

Forgive me Lord
For my desire
For power, to change
Unloveliness.
Come Holy Spirit
Come Lord Jesus
My Joy and
My Cross.
Your Will
Your Grace
Prevail. Amen

This prose was also written on the 27th November:

'During the day, I was seeking to praise, bless and fulfil the things that needed to be done despite the fatigue of my body- but meanwhile staying with the sense of loss and pain of the cross – and yet the Silence of Christ on the Cross;

I sense awesome nothingness – and without prayer I can do nothing – without praise I am nothing.

When I threatened to sink into nothingness, I sensed God saying He wanted/needed me to overcome *'the nations' and be for Him a light in the darkness.'*

28th November 2012

In the half awake state this morning I sensed the Lord saying, '*Woman – your son'* – I believe – Lord help me - this is the writer in me– the bearer of the Word – in and with me.

Oh Lord, Your will be done – Your Kingdom come.

I have, since 21st November, been getting up for prayer downstairs – but still spending time with God in bed before this; I sense now (prompted by St Marina?) I must get up for these times of intimacy and overcome my desire to be nurtured and TRUST God with it. (Dear Reader, this reflects my growing awareness of my desire to be nurtured, but shifting the responsibility for this from a human level of 'comfort' – to trust that God will provide through Prayer.)

(After the prose above)

Glory

On the cross
Arms stretched wide
My Lord.
Dead to sin
From conception,
He gave all
For all,
In obedience
To His Father.

Writing

Write My darling daughter
All I have taught you,
All I have bought you,
The life, the cross,
The tomb, the resurrection.*
You are Mine-
And I am yours.

Glory to You
Oh Holy, Holy, Holy Lord.
Your will be done
My Beloved.
May I follow You
My God.

*Lord I believe, help Thou my unbelief.
Oh Lord, I confess my half-heartedness-
That I have not believed – have
run away from this intimacy
and 'work'- seeking pleasure
and ease in this life.
I confess my lack of love,
Lord have mercy.

*Let me be raised in You Lord –
'Speaking the truth in Love'. Amen.

June 22 2022

In obedience and in order to underline what the Holy Spirit had provided in my spiritual 'travels' of the previous 23 years, was building on through these 'listening's', and the acceptance of the pain and happenings of my childhood, I add to the original journals from Wales.

At this time in Wales, I did not know a great deal about 'trauma' and the effects on the brain and all the research that has now been done. Back in 1990 after I had first given my life to Christ, I spent 5 months going to a psychiatric day hospital after exhaustion led me to let go of my work in higher education. At the end of that time, I had reached the point where I was able to face some painful memories, without 'dying', and subsequently had been on at least 4 residential Christian healing conferences on Inner Healing'. The Holy Spirit had revealed at least an outline of some of my childhood events and circumstances re: parent relationships which I had not 'known', being illegitimate for example, and self-hatred as a woman.

I had received much prayer at church. and in other healing contexts. This had started to soften my hardness of heart towards myself, and I began to know that I needed God, and I had the beginning of trust. At one evening healing conference I had 'claimed' my healing. .... So, God took me at my Word, and led me to let go of my 'invalidity benefit!! I think this was the first time that a 'reality' wall was broken down in a very real way. If I was believing what Christ had done – I needed to act as if I did!! In integrity, I couldn't have both the Healing and the Invalidity Benefit!!.

And I had started to live out the healing – following the way I was led – but part of the growth in maturity was a renewal of my mind which had to face the damage and broken mind sets arising from trauma!

So in the years preceding this retreat to Wales, I had started reading a book on Memory and Abuse. This had helped me accept the effects of trauma, and integrate an understanding of the damage suffered, with Christ's teaching and healing. Christ's healing was very 'practical' and worked from the inside and through 'expansion' of the Inner Being of what had been shut down, through Action and the Holy Spirit. Thus, through God's Grace changing my lifestyle and purpose, my heart and mind were 'expanded' and changed not simply through 'intellectual' understanding of it, but through being and acting. See the prayer of Jabez – so crucial for trauma sufferers. (1 Chronicles 4:9-10) – 'Lord Extend my boundaries, that You may be with me….'

So here I was 23 years later being encouraged to share the truth of what He had taught me.

Essentially, I had learned to let go of trying to control everybody and everything but learn to control myself - and thus, embrace living by the Spirit. I had overcome the narrowness of my 'life' by returning to the 'art' of my school years which I had let go of when offered a place on the Physical Education course for teacher training. I had accepted God's call to places I did not know and learned to trust God's provision.

I overcame the fear of being judged in order to become an artist and creator of Calendars which spread the Word and Life of Christ; I had learned to accept being on my own with Christ and His Word, without fear; I had learned many manifestations of Life in the Body of Christ, seeing Him in all the 'denominations' I had lived and worked with. I had found the tenderness of God in His 'mothering' not simply through Mary the Mother of God, but also through the simple 'family' provision of l'Abri in Switzerland, or the kindness of Theresa in Switzerland; and I became open to all the 'natural' and super-natural manifestations of His love… in simple 'loving friendship' that works miracles; and the miracle manifestations of weeping icons, for example, or carrying my car up a road of sheet ice, which normally needed snow-chains.

In all the above He was providing new life, hope and 'reality' for my traumatised heart/ brain, which had seen danger in everything and only by working things out and being 'in control' could I act. I had no colour in my childhood memories, except the fire which I sometimes would sit by at night when I had toothache, and the blue and green of a baby memory when lying in my pram outside. The Lord 'restored my soul'….and gave me colour and form, as I learned to draw and use colour. These are not often spoken of in 'spiritual development', but without the 'restoration of the soul', how can we commit ourselves to God who was fully human and divine? It is only half a decision if we do not allow Him to challenge and change our 'lifelessness'!!

I had had no problem with the 'tough love' of being purified and sanctified within the Orthodox Church, but God was wanting me to move on to stand on Higher ground within my own understanding of Life in Christ – the next step meant letting go of all 'childish thinking' about my Life in Christ as I move into maturity. So having learned forgiveness and repentance and humanity in life, I needed to know more about LOVE.

4

Overcoming Intransigence:

Shifting Understanding to Higher Ground

SPIRITUAL WARFARE...

Glory II

Hidden in the Holy Heart
Lies a seed hidden in the ground.
Life stirs like a Promise
Watered by Love, Prayer,
Hope and God honouring life-
Hidden, without will-
Growing without expectation
Holiness in Christ alone.
Amen.
Overcoming death, lies, defeat
Day by day.
Amen.

Glory III

Dying,
Living,
Loving,
Forgiving,
Forbearing,
But speaking
The Truth in Love.

P.S. Again- non-delivery of expected goods - And I didn't go to Mary's because of the cold, and weariness of my body - And I battled and stumbled through the day bearing the cross of unknowing and loss - the heaviness of the work of the course and the weight of unhealed 'masculine authority', triggering a hurting heart.

29th November 2012

06.30

Death

I wake in my body
With no desire for good -
yet I will praise You my God.

My heart is heavy and weary
with no hope for life-
Yet I will praise You my God.

My thoughts are selfish
and inward turning-
yet I will praise You my God.

Why? My God, how long my God
will you turn your back on me?
Yet I will praise You my God.
(As I allowed the darkness of defeat and despair to emerge and yet praised, the heaviness lifted and acceptance and willingness to persevere took over-Glory to God.)

Selfishness Redeemed

Self hating, tyrannical
Undenied desire for life
Transformed by the cross
Into purity of heart
And search for the Living God.

Beloved

Oh my Beloved, have mercy on me
Your servant. Let me hear you
with clarity; a willing heart,
a loving spirit hidden in You -
that You live in me . One for God
Reluctant to serve

My body is weary, tired
And reluctant to serve,
Claiming its rest and gentleness.
But there are souls to save and
All other tasks there for Friday –

And my body knows it must comply
Or rest in hell, alone
Joyless, faithless, without love.

But yet she calls out to You my God
Oh my God why have You abandoned me?
All I wanted was comfort,
Gentleness, blessed assurance.
Forgive me my God for my intransigence
Forgive me for not trusting you.
Oh my God have mercy on me.

Allowance

Given to God at birth -
Struggling to overcome
Through the one who saves –
In the grave with Him
Fighting for life
Without joy or visible hope
To sustain. Forgive them

The Invisible Wall

Patriarchy - righteousness
But without love
When it refuses to lift
Enable, honour God given gifts,
And make the Church
Fulfilling what Christ came for.
To save souls.

So the invisible wall
Cuts off the saving Grace
And Unity in Christ
From those outside
The brotherhood of priests.
Have men lost the
Apostolic gift
to act in the Spirit
except at the altar?
And God's action thus confined
To a building and a time-
And the invisible wall
Holds Him in
Keeping Him from life.

-

Precious in My sight

Like a lamb given to slaughter
so are you in My sight.
A precious ewe lamb
sacrificed for the life of many.

I will not leave you, or for sake you.
I will provide for your needs -
even today child.
I will bind up your wounds
and heal your broken heart.
Your mind is weary -
come to me, and forgive them
for their intransigence, hard heartedness
and self interest.
Forgive them and pray for them they know not what they do.
Pride cannot provide for them, or you,
But the Holy Spirit will reprove,
Heal, and purify them.

Yes child, you are precious in My sight.

30th November 2012

07:20

Gentleness

It was late, last night, my Lord
when work and prayer stopped,
Though You warned me it would be,
And now my mind
Wants to claim more sleep
For this loveless weary body.
But my Lord there is much
To pray and do before we leave.
By Your Love I ask your Grace,
Truth, Beauty and Gentleness
To persevere - to the glory of God.

P.S. Because I was so late getting up I was blessed with a shortened Matins (but including kathisma) and then the day was fruitful in grace - table tidied, emails re: calendars written and sent, and Contacts on Facebook notified, four calendars packaged with notes and posted - long phone call to City Link re the parcel. Conversations with people - but above all peace in Christ. Thank You- to You alone be glory.

(NOTE - I found from the small red journal that I went to Cardiff to see my sister, and took her to see my brother, and to visit my son and family in their new home. On the 2nd I was still in her flat but came back the 3rd Dec ....thus.............)

4th December 2012

07:33

Hopelessness

Promises once more unmet
and yesterday, twice promised,
No phone was connected;
And in my heart - death.
Yet God gave me grace to
Study Isaiah and consider
Your word God to the exiled Jews.
Let nothing of this world
be an Idol for me -
but where are you my God ?
How do I go on in exile
With no means of contact?
Yet you give me grace
and I will praise you -
Holy, holy, holy God -
I worship you.

Overcoming

'Overcoming death by death
And on those in the tombs
Bestowing life.'*
So be it my God -
I believe, help Thou
My unbelief.

*This is a quote from the Troparion for the Resurrection

Waiting

anger, bitterness
sadness, loss
lie in the tomb
of my heart
waiting, hoping
for someone
to come and rescue.

Open door

I open the heart-door Lord
to let You in
to this pit of misery
And hopelessness.
Why did You do it?
Why did You come
*Why did You let me
Suffer like this?
Why did You allow
This descent to hell?

I have no answer
to this rational mind.
Have mercy on me a Sinner.
Lord Jesus by Your Light
I will see.

I have silenced this voice -
Who wants to raise
These questions to you-
my God -
Why did You let it happen -To the child?
In my head I think I know the answer -
For your greater glory *-
But I sense no glory here.
Because I fall with the cross -
And I'm fighting
Against this stillness and loss. Come Lord Jesus -
Come Holy Spirit.

I believe, help me Beloved
Overcome this 'rational'
Complaint and death .

*Only in May 2022 did God give me an answer to this question – when I had faced and confessed a deep rooted hatred of God for 'allowing' this death by my stepfather. God made it clear He did not 'allow' it – i.e. give permission for it, but He has given free will to man-kind and without going against Himself, and because I was powerless as a child, it happened. This also illustrates how our deep and complex traumas need to 'unfold' and we need to trust God with the right timing. 'Your Will be done'.

5th December 2012

Reflection

I know I cannot change myself - but last night I sensed, in my unutterable death/hopelessness that I was more integrated - complete - in a reality of not running away. Even death on the Cross. What wonder of grace!! What a gift!!

I sensed the abuse of broken promises - I know the grace Christ gives to overcome the privation of this place day by day - but I sensed the truth of the sense of loss and total powerlessness to do anything about it. This in itself was empowering to my soul.

As a child, it must have been the same - no one came to my cries, no one listened to what I told them - at least that's how it seemed, and no one listens now in the church to women - except to condemn those who have followed the open door in the Church of England.

I have promised God to be faithful to Him in the Orthodox Church - but I am wilfully not doing the assignment as set as it doesn't make any sense to me. Obedience is a keyword in Orthodoxy. Am I obedient to man or my Holy conscience or a God who does not speak?

Is it my conscience or a broken heart that is guiding me?
Come Holy Spirit ……..

Reassignment

I can't see what it matters about the biographical details of Isaiah - only how and what God spoke – (Surely man is wanting to judge man – Are we capable?)

Also, if we focus on simply the exilic Jews we missed the message for us today. God was, is and is to come - shouldn't we hear this?

If I do not stand with what is in my Heart I die again - but I need you my God to confirm because if I do not speak the truth in Love then no one will hear and there is no value anyway.

And in speaking, I risk being shot down with all their Cleverness, because they do not ask me to explain

What they do not understand.

Oh Lord give me courage and love.
Gentleness and patience
humility and grace
TO STAND, AND YET STAND
IN HARMONY within with you.

JESUS

Holy One of God,
MY ALL in all
My Hope, Salvation,
Joy and Love-
I surrender
To Your Cross
All the bitterness
And misery
Of this place
And I accept
What You provide.
I have told You -
You cannot choose me,
To bear Your burdens,
To carry Your Word
To forgive the unforgivable-
But You have.
I accept Your call
on my life -
my life / Your life.
Have mercy on me a Sinner.
Gentle Judge – prends pitiez*.

Oh my God, why have you abandoned me?
Have courage gentle one
To persevere in grace and faith
Praise and thanksgiving
One step at a time.
Do the washing,
Make your cards,
Prepare the shed-

Make your phone calls (BT, Kath, Sylvia)
Bless and uphold those you encounter.
*COURAGE **is** a light in the darkness.*

*French for 'Have Mercy".

6th December 2012

'Last night found Priest-Monk Silouan* had left a message asking when he should come to do the blessing of the cottage, and also informing me that according to the website I am still living at the island monastery.

I no longer have the strength to fight or make bold decisions. My God – Your will be done – Let me pray'

Yours

My life is yours
but the battle goes on
surrendering the flesh
To You - overcoming
Death, desire for love,
Wanting something
Getting nothing
Yet everything through You.

Yours II

I am yours
I have promised
That I will never leave
Or forsake you.
Into Eternity!!
Never forget My Name
Jesus, the Holy One of God
Redeemer and friend.
Justice is Mine
Says the Lord.

Amen Amen Amen.
I in you, you in Me
And I in the Father -
Come Holy Spirit.

7th December 2012

Confusion

In this darkness
I do not see Your face
I do not know Your voice
I am without choice.

Yet my God
You have promised
You will be with me
Though I sink to the depths.

So I praise You for your mercy
I praise You for your love
In faith and hope
I trust in Your Love to love.

Although by God's mercy things were done - I failed to get up early and felt everything had gone back to square one - though eventually I was obedient, to prayer rule of matins and kathisma and vespers. Did eventually get quotes into 5 minute talk for Saturday at the Course, and through divine Providence a couple who came to look at the end cottage took the microwave and needed the stainless steel cooking pans. And prior to seeing them, in looking to see if I could get rid of the microwave at the recycling in the car park, I found a small lamp to use as an outside light in the window when I go out with the dog at night. Thank you, Lord for Your providential provision, and mercy and grace to persevere. Give me Grace and courage to fight this fight –

Courage darling of My Heart
to face truth and loss
And overcome in My Name
And through My Word. Amen

Monogamy

This place* is without gentleness
yet You have made it gentle-
It is without love
yet You have made it loving.
It is without future
and only knows the past.

Let me work
to purify your broken heart
And mind -
to bring all bitterness
To the Cross -
all loss turned to fruitfulness.

*This place refers to the 'cottage' (one room downstairs and shower room and bedroom upstairs) I am living in. But it could refer to my human heart too.

In prayer: ***Forgiveness is for when someone repents:***
Prior to that they are our 'enemies' and therefore need prayer and blessing –

Oh Lord hear my prayer –

Thank you for this wisdom and Truth.

10Th December 2012

The alarm went off at 6:00 AM, an hour later I got up and made a cup of tea and got my vitamins and came back to bed. Read two psalms and some of the gospel then went to sleep. I tried to overcome this tiredness and despair and sense of no future. I didn't want to write a poem - yet I know God is with me - so, forgive me, Lord.

08:50

Unwanted

Given life by God
But unwanted:
given birth by God
but unwanted.

It happened then
it's happening now.
A woman
who doesn't fit the plan,
the structure made by man.

But they say it's Yours
My God, so I have
No fight.
'Cause how can I fight You?
So give me grace
To accept
This death.
Take my will to love and live for You
and trust You.
Oh my God why have you abandoned me?
Give me grace to love and trust you.
In Jesus Name, Amen

P.S. Praying – and overcoming, but prayer in tears. We have so much to repent of – oh dear God have mercy on us.

(Whenever I pray in repentance, I am blessed with the Light of Christ showing me my own darkness, pride, bitterness, and also self-condemning because I am not simply turning to Christ in faith.)

11th December 2012

The devil calls me 'c...face' and 'f...-head' in the darkness, and my mind has lost hope in places 'where no birds sing'. But I must 'keep my mind in hell and not despair'* and I believe and trust that in Christ all manner of things will be well. I simply pray that this agony of despairing and broken-mind will be purified and healed through repentance in Christ. (*St Silouan had been unable to worship Christ because the devil kept getting in the way. Eventually, he was told this was to do with his pride, so he needed to 'keep his mind in hell but not despair'. I had been given St Silouan as a protecting saint at Chrismation when I was received into the Orthodox church.)
'Dogma" – What does it mean*? It means having to obey other people's knowledge of God – Until each has knocked, asked, and sought and found and received for themselves.*

Lies

The devil names
The acts of abuse
And makes them
My name.

But Christ's death
And crucifixion -
The wounds and
Lacerations

Are not His truth -
Yet by His wounds
We are healed
Made whole.

So every abuse
Accepted and surrendered
Forgiven and blessed
Brings hope –
Every loss
Of the cross
Is gain in Him
And frees the soul.

Confusion

Made clarity
In forgiveness
And love.

Your work
My God-
In poverty
Surrendered

I was listening to the darkness within:
Shame
Bitterness
Despair

Loss of life Becomes
Hope and
purity of heart

I bless him Lord.

Have mercy on me and him.

<u>Strongholds to be broken open</u>
Self Protection
Self healing
Denial of pain and loss
Rebellion against Authority
Lack of trust in Authority
Seeking comfort

I confess my sin, dear Father, and through Christ my Lord, ask for purification and healing.

Let all this vainglory cease – Oh dear God please provide through my commitment to You.

12th December 2012

07:45

Commitment

Committed to you my God
Yet I have been running away
Not believing - not wanting
Your voice or spirit.

Now I see my sin
My worldly desires for comfort,
Courage to overcome -
When if I received
Your will and purpose
There would be no struggle.

"Darling, dearest of My heart
Have courage to step
Into the Black Hole of Love
And find My Presence
Love, Justice, Truth
And Beauty. "

Amen Lord, Amen.

I put into your hands
The worldly happenings of today
Truth and grace
In repentance for the sins of the world -
and love for You.
"And I for you "
Thank you - glory to You my God.

Write Paint LOVE.

I will commit to You and Your task.

(I had to take the car to be serviced this morning and they ran me up to Mary's so I could work with her this morning. Car still not ready when Harry drove me down so I wrote cards at the vegetarian cafe (Mulberry Bush). Glory to God.

Fighting despair and yet resting in His Presence in my heart and had peace.

I had grace to pray at Vespers and was delivered from more despair and evil in my gut - felt the pain in my gut. Come Lord Jesus.

Lord I look to you but how/what do I serve you?
WRITE your Name – 'Emmanuel' - God is with us.
Seraphima

-God the Father
'I am angry at the men of the church who serve for their own glory - but not Mine -
not for My Purposes - for the impure who need Salvation.'

Forgive your mother who knew not what she did – (re feeding and not holding me for many years).

Forgive your mother for her lack of love for you –

I asked if I must write and heard *'Of course you must write, bearer of God the Word.'*

Blessed are those who mourn for they will be comforted.

"I am despised and rejected in the church, 'a man of grief and acquainted with sorrows' a man from whom men turn their heads.'

"Where have my good shepherds gone? Into hiding from bishops who do not want My Will or Life.

Do not think that I can overcome like with like. My good shepherds suffer with Me, as you do, they await a miracle and answered prayer – (And I added 'that we may be one in You')-*NO child, that the Body would accept its function - to SAVE SOULS.*

You are my body here on earth - Driven by lust for power everyone works for themselves -but driven by my Spirit in love - all work for each other and the lost. (Lord have mercy)

20:13

Running Away

I'm running away
from the mess downstairs
washing up not done,
table untidy and disordered.

But the internet connexion is not functioning
And I am called to be still -
And with God-
Face the mess
Of my life
Face the disordered soul
Still crying out for a mother
And rescue from the abuse.

Yet in Christ
is peace,
Hope and purification.
But this death surrounded me,*
Like the psalmist says-
And my soul is lost
in this darkness -

Still running away
From the awesome loss -
And the glory of God.

*Psalm 17:5

21st June 2022

(God stepped in while I was writing up.)
Child, you are looking for outward
Recognition of My Grace
to lift you
From this pit of death.
Make this pit My birthing place
O glory -turn every darkness
To Eternal Life and Let Me
Live in You.
Lord I feel this Truth - Amen

Lord have mercy on me -
Help me trust in embracing
This darkness - where no birds sing.
Functional, enough, ugly
No attractive appearance -
This cottage – a whited sepulchre.
And me- dark within-.

(In the night led to pray the Psalms - but reluctant to stay up long - though my heart was filled with consolation –)

13th December 2012

Then this morning fought a battle to get up……

Mine

Child of darkness, born in pain
Child of promise, born again
You are Mine - the holy one
My child, my daughter
Well beloved.
Let me uphold, deliver
Bless and honour you
With my love.
Trust me to protect
from all harm
Gentle spirit - come.

Jesus envelop me
My Lord and my God.
Forgive me.

The love and gentleness and promise of the above words brought to light the fear behind my reluctance to serve and pray.

Lord Jesus Christ have mercy on me a sinner.

14th December 2012

I have been continuing to read 'The Heart of Salvation- the Life and Teachings of Saint Theophan the Recluse' - and the last chapters are about being before God - and in His Presence, all worldly concerns and pleasures flee away and we remain in awareness of Him - no longer desiring distractions.

Oh dear God -let it be so. Let nothing distract me from You - I have been kicking and screaming at this desert here - with no phone and no distraction! Oh Papa - forgive me - thank you for the tribulations and crosses you have brought me through. Awesome God - glorious Lord - divine Spirit - I love and desire you.

Glory

As mouse before a lion
or molehill by a mountain
my nothingness before you
is beautiful truth.

I surrender all vainglory
to the beauty of Your Love.
I accept this holy blackness
And walk in faith, hope and love.

Surrender my precious one
All your hopes, plans and
lust for power, to the Cross
And let me be your God.

You are without power
because you have destroyed yourself
in order to create My Life
My Love, My Purposes.

You have given yourself
for a greater good
To save souls and to love
For My glory.

You have taken My Word
and made it yours
you are Mine My child
With all your gifts in My hand.

(After days of frost and ice - today it is raining again and the dripping outside foretells a wet dog and muddy feet. Lord, give me the grace to forebear!)

5

Overcoming Intransigence

Accepting Life Hidden in Christ in God

14th December 2012

Friends of God

Child, beloved of the Father,
Penance is over. Rejoice
At every trial
Do not be sorry for yourself
But confess your Saviour -
Jesus Christ is Lord
Jesus Christ is the holy one
Jesus Christ pierces the darkness
By the piercing of his wounds –
So no darkness remains so,
When surrendered to the cross.
Rest in trust in the Father's love
At all times.
Glory to God alone.
Saving souls with every forgiving,
loving breath.

No Grace can overcome death.
Only the Heart of the Father.
Only perfection in Love.

Suffering

I have brought you through
Your losses as a child
Into the greyness in which you lived,
Powerlessness, comfortless, hopeless –
And yet I sustained you in hope.
And I show you the tragedy
Of the cross - the loss and suffering
In all things truly human -
In loss of life, separated from Me.
But only to forgive and redeem,
And in Me know My Life and Hope for you in Christ .

My Will not yours be done

Your defeat child is My door -
Be glad in your defeat in the church -
I open doors:
I call you to Me
Obedience to Me
For love of all the Church.

My silence is blessed
But I need to speak to you
Do not be afraid.

*Memory will be unblocked***
That you may love Me
With all your heart and mind
And soul and strength.

According to My Word.
I need you to know
The extent of My Grace
Working in and through you.
TRUST and seek My heart
In all things.
I am your strength.

Do NOT worry
About what you eat or drink
From this day forward
Give thanks in all things.

** Only in writing this up did I understand God's promise here. You will see how God does this restoring of memory in Book II of the Trilogy (Healing the Broken Hearted)
'Your Will be Done: Beyond Powerlessness and Fear – Revelation of Life in Love'.

15 December 2012

Sacred sorrow

I woke before the alarm
But too late for midnight prayer,
My willingness when I slept.

But the shadow overweighed me
And though I got up to make a tea
No will for good grew fruit in me.
And in prayer I slept again.

And now more refreshed I seek
The face of Him lowly and meek
Who gives me hope and life
Amid the sorrow of this strife -

The greyness of my childhood years
Threatens more unholy tears
As I live again abandonment
And neglect of love.

The cares of the world
Lay heavy last night
As tempted to sin by another
He heaped on me his burdens.

And in love I must act,
But Father I still trust in You
And Your divine love and truth
To guide him, lead him and provide for him.

And meanwhile Your Word
Tells me You will not ask
More of me than I can do or suffer
With the Grace and Love of You.

I want to scream and shout of injustice - and all the bitterness of the psalmist who sees the carelessness and richness of those who live in the world and deny God (Psalm 52)

Oh my beloved Lord, glorious Father I cannot deny You without denying the wonder of what You have done for me and carried me through.

I saw again 'writing' on a previous page and understand even more what you have done. But I have no clarity of thought without You.

Will you enable me if I give myself to you - give time?

"No child - it is not necessary. You can do it in My Name. One God -One Lord, One Spirit - the human with the divine united in purpose to glorify God."

Lord I believe - help thou my unbelief.

Child - they destroyed your life, love, hope and will for good. You believed in My unity and oneness in Christ and the church - this is the 'sacred sorrow' of your poem. You see no way to go - no purpose in your life - no one seeking your good.

You are alive in Christ - and that Christ crucified. Dead to the pleasures of the world - alive to the sorrow for sin and compassion for the lost and broken hearted for whom you can only pray.

Forgive your mother for never giving you her love for you in right ways. For never honouring your gifts or talents, for never promoting or disciplining / encouraging you in the flesh, i.e. in human ways.

Gifted

I sense neglected, even unwrapped gifts
Lie at the foot of the cross
Unloved, untouched, neglected
not watered or honoured.
Lord Jesus Christ have mercy.

And the body is like lifeless
Dead works on the cross
Without hope, vision
Or purpose - as abandoned
By all, there is no love.

Lord may I start the task
You have given me -
to write the gifts You
Have given me in
My life - and use the
Gifts that lie abandoned
that they be liveable
And without shame?

Come Lord Jesus.
Come Holy Spirit

17TH December 2012

Waiting

The darkness waits
round every corner
pouncing on hesitations
and underlining
every lovelessness.

Come Lord Jesus
Bind me to your Holy Spirit
In Thanksgiving, Praise,
And eternal gratitude
To the Heart that saves.

Thank you Holy Father
That You have not destroyed me-
Thank You that I have Grace
To turn to You in openness
And desire to love You.

Thank you that even
in the dark of death
Your light shines -
The Cross illuminating
All.

Thank You for the beauty
All around
and that I create through You
Or You create through me!?
Thank You for eyes to see-

And ears to hear
And heart to love.
Thank you for the many sisters
Brothers and friends I have
Through You. Glory to You.

But Jesus holy Lord
Take this day for Your purpose.
Take my hands, feet,
Tongue and heart
To move to Your rhythm
And speak and beat for
Your redemptive purposes.
I love you Jesus.

18th December 2012

Heaviness, sloth, despair weighs me down and threatens death.
But last night I stood and let You carry me through redoing
the room curtains and preparing rods and finding material
for the bedroom and other kitchen curtains. Glory to God

PS - and during the morning I completed the tasks and put the curtains to wash so now (18 / 12 /12) they are all in place including a separate curtain for the Chapel corner. Glory to God.

Gentleness

Embraced in the love of God
Overcoming all death,
The Spirit of God softens
All intentions
To become, like a butterfly,
Gentle wing-beats
In God's heart -
Like molten gold
Poured into a mould
Leaving a footprint
Of the Lord.

All actions softened,
Purified and cleansed
From stain,
And they simply are -In God.
All embraced in His love -
Grace, truth, honesty -
Delivered from the stain of sin
Delivered from the hatred of satan
Or the lies of the world.
Delivered my darling daughter
From men's intransigence.

Beloved

This fasting body is weak
But You are strong my Lord.
Give me strength for the day
And wisdom to know whether
To break the fast for the journey
Tomorrow night.

Oh Beloved I am so dependent
On You. My confidence
Is in You alone.   Amen, Amen.

Gentleness II

Gentleness and trust
Will carry you through
All trials.

Oh Lord deliver me
From all disinterest
And unwillingness to serve
Or to act for a greater good.

Hidden heart

I want to hide away
To cover myself and rest
And to open my heart
To be in You with You
Without a body.
But You became Incarnate
And in me You need this body
To serve and bless -
Lord Your will not mine be done.

I lay down after reading about an on-line campaign's actions and successful change and I was weeping inside and did not believe I could take action to change things: as a child in order to stop the abuse or change the effects; or now -in the church.. Lord, Your Way is my desire but let me see and know Your will. Am I mistaken in believing what St Paul says,.". *In Christ is neither male nor female….*"

Power I

Oh my beloved,
Even pinioned on a cross
You forgave your persecutors -
Those who killed you -
Despised You - persecuted You
And said all manner of evil against you.

You forgave -
You in your humanity forgave
Because you knew the Father loved You
And Your worth did not rely on their actions.
Jesus, lover of my soul,
Let me enter deep into Your Heart
And You into mine
That I may know my Father's
Love for me through You.

Then I can stand, and yet stand-
And forgive as You forgave -
Yet my Lord I cry out for justice
In the church that Your prayer
May be fulfilled.

I cry out for the lost and broken
Who You love, who do not hear the Word -
Oh Papa don't let me be deceived -
Take all double mindedness from me
Because of the deceit and loss of the Cross.

Power II

Gentleness through the cross
Pinioned - not able to move,
Yet saving the world!
So be it my Lord, my God.
So be it my Father.
So be it Holy Spirit.
No death for God.
No death but Resurrection.
Into Your hands
I commit my spirit.

Your Will be done.

Jabez II

Born in pain and loss
Upheld by unseen hands
Purified in heart and mind
By Guardian Angels -
Yet in manhood
Crying out to God -
"Father, bless me."
Years of pain and loss
Uprooted at a glance
From the Eyes that save
And forgive.

Blessing

All reluctance, bitterness and faithlessness
Melts before Your Beauty and Truth.
Truly You are the overcoming one –
And I accept this tomb of a cottage.

Yesterday through necessity I found
That I could see the treetops and birds
And sky - by looking upwards
From the bedroom window.
I was lifted in my spirit when I sensed
St Cuthbert reminding me of his cell
Which only looked upwards.
I had accepted this place on that basis –
with my head –
But with my heart it's been difficult
As landscape had been my consolation.

Dear God - you have asked me to write what you have given me - I don't do it yet but I don't know how. Words - and rational thought are so inadequate - but I haven't even tried. Do you want me to try?

"No beloved of my heart LOVE this into being. "

Oh dear God I love you because you always give me puzzles that You then have to clarify for me!!

"Dependence on My ways and being."

I was praying about On-Line campaigns:

"Political correctness is a misnomer-

a) there is no correctness in God's eyes because there is no pure love and concern for the soul or well being of the person;

b) politics is to do with power and denies responsibilities because it simply demands status without concern for God's Kingdom."

19th December 2012

08:10

The Redeemer

The Redeemer works in me
To do the will of the Father,
Yet the unredeemed in me
Pulls like an undercurrent
Against His flow and my being in Him.
Yet Lord I look to you
And trust this work
That You have started.

Honesty -

I am torn my Lord
between the thoughts
That return me to be near
The place of original
Commitment to you in Nailsea
Or to return to Scotland
To Dunblane which Father Silouan
Had discerned
And later my spirit wanted,
And now Father M has texted.
That seems like Father, Son
And Holy Spirit all witnessing
To the same thing.
Lord I believe, help thou
My unbelief .

But you called me for the church*
So I say 'Your will be done'.
And I choose for this witness
That you have given me.
Accepting this way of the cross,
Prepared before hand to Your
Praise and glory.

* This was confirmed when I found myself at Sourati Monastery (near Thessaloniki) for the Feast of the Entry of the Theotokos to the Temple in 2013.

Calling

I am calling you out
To a place of resurrection
Commitment to life in Christ
A life of love, gentleness
Compassion and grace.
Poverty and fullness,
Justice and beauty
All given by God.
This is My word to you
My promise to you.
My love for you.
Daughter - yes Lord
Love me with all your heart,
Mind and strength
And do not be afraid

I will give you strength
For today - tonight -
Tomorrow and till you return.*
You have sufficient funds
For your needs. (I had tried to calculate!).

*BT are coming to install the phone- Christmas packing and cleaning – drive to the island overnight – Bill Pollocks' funeral and loading car with tyres and stuff from church – then to Edinburgh, then home on Sunday 23rd.

I am the handmaid of the Lord

My beloved - I desire with all my heart
To love You with my all -
Please help me do that.
I pray in all humility
I love, help Thou my lack of love.
I adore and praise You –
Yet I weep my dear One
That You should love me.
I trust, help Thou my lack of trust.
Build me my God
In goodness and truth
To your praise and glory.
Forgive me for my lack of love.
Child –(I listened)
Your littleness is a stumbling block
To those who are blind -
Your patience and desire for My ways
An impediment to those who do not know Me,
But to Me they are My open door -
Where My grace can abound
And bear fruit.

Do not imagine child, any future
Or any facet, but patiently trust,
Praise and call on My Name.
I will deliver you from all self harming.
Holiness befits my Saints.
*(*Lord I believe, help thou my unbelief -
I desire patience beyond measure,
Love without restraint - oh Jesus
My Lord and God I love you. *)*
"I am sending you child in My Name – be blessed."

From 'Heart of Compassion' – Daily Readings with St Isaac of Syria. Ed. AM Allchin, P.37:

'Someone who bears a grudge as he or she prays is like a person who sows in the sea and expects to reap a harvest'.

'As the flame of a fire cannot be prevented from ascending upwards, so the prayers of the compassionate cannot be held back from ascending to heaven'.

Lord I forgive, help thou any unforgiveness or hardness of heart. You died on the cross and asked the Father to forgive - heavenly Father please forgive and heal my wounds.

Today

The beginning -
Today the phone will be installed
In My name, for My purposes -
Not to keep you amused child!
I have harrowed you afresh
And you have been obedient -
Glory to God -
Humbled, pure, holy,
Patient in trials.
Compassionate in all things

Humbled before God.

Let My voice of Thanksgiving
Be heard on the island-
Gracious gratitude
For this holy provision.
In unholy environment
Do not be ashamed
Of your hatred of the 'wall' -
Let the victim acknowledge the truth
I will give you grace to overcome.

The wall

Lord the wall is like
The apparent wall built
Against me/women in the church
so I cannot see a way.
But I will praise, give thanks
And put my trust in You. +

(My heart has accepted its response to the wall in front of me - physically and emotionally /spiritually in the church - yet I will trust and know that my Lord will overcome with me - as I praise and thank God for the courage He gives me to praise Him and forbear.

Jesus I love you . *darling of My heart have courage.'*

The Wall (continued in new journal…)

-By prayer and Your spirit
I've found myself blessing the wall -
That is in front of the cottage
but also the wall constructed
By misogyny and lies
against women in the church.
Oh dear Lord Your Love
Overcomes - I bless in Your Name
these walls because they are enemies
And stumbling blocks to the faithful.

Unless there is Unity
In love, there will be no growth
Or life in the Orthodox Church.
Facing the unseen real -
The devil divides -
The Holy Spirit unites.

23rd December 2012 On the island.

I wake and pray the Jesus prayer in hope while my body lies in the battlefield of despair and loss of life. –

Only you Lord give me Grace to even cling to prayer and desire for You. I love You.

Anguish and Loss

Sharp anguish pangs
Pierce my mind
with lies of despair.
My heart empty of love,
Hope empty of direction.

But yet my God I lean
On you. Trust in You
And praise You for all
You have brought me through.
I confess my sin and lack of faith.

I put Jane's needs my Beloved
Into Your hands. Have mercy on her.
May her birthday be blessed*.

I stand in Your Holy Name
Against this apparent lovelessness
And self hatred.
And I look to You.
To Your grace alive in me -
And my trust in Your Love.

***the 23rd of December is my older half-sister's birthday.**

Wales

Come Lord Jesus ,
come Holy Spirit
transform this death and darkest night
To grace and truth and love
By Your fruitfulness and fulness.

Child - beloved of the Father –
Your simple trust and faith to overcome
-Is a star in the darkness –
A jewel in your Father's hand.
Pray for Jay and Jenny and all women
Abandoned by men and society in their youth.
I love you daughter - beyond measure.
You are mine. And I am yours.
One God, One Lord, one Spirit.
Do not be afraid of the apparent unknowing
About your return to Wales –
Your sense of uncertainty about everything you do
Before you do it.
Humility and faith, trust and hope in Me –
God the Father through Christ and the Holy Spirit.

22nd December 2012 **(**Staying at M's in Edinburgh)

Works

Works prepared beforehand -
To see M and S,
To talk gently and purely
With my hostess
With trust in the Holy Spirit
Of Unity and Purpose.

Holiness my daughter
A dwelling place
For worship
Trust, obedience to the Spirit,
Work in creativity
Prayer, order -
Justice and love. Amen

I will trust In God's purposes
for this journey to Scotland
and stand against the threat
of defeat, fear and fatigue.
To God be the glory as I rest in Him.
Glory to You my God.
In spirit and in truth I will worship you.

23rd December 2012

Resurrection day

He is risen the woman cried,
Stony hearted the men did not believe,
But finally run to the tomb
To see for themselves.
The Truth, they had denied.
Ignoring the woman
And every woman
Who has cried, He is risen.
Hard-hearted, bent to themselves
They do not believe
That the woman carried
The word of God.
He is risen indeed.

In gentleness and prayer
Purity, Trust and Love.
In patient forbearance
Eyes on the Father
Looking, interceding, waiting,
Hoping - come Lord Jesus, come.
Come and heal our wounds
And divisions. Come.

Prayer

Always, in all situations
Interceding, standing in the gap.
Father forgive them they know not
What they do.
Have mercy on us. Have mercy on us
To You alone be glory

Knowing the unknowable
Seeing the unseeable
Acknowledging the unacknowledgeable.
I bow before You and worship You my God

Have faith child
That in all circumstances I will lead and guide you,
Uphold and enflesh you in all mildness, gentleness and truth.
I will provide a way in the darkness of unknowing.
You see with My eyes and heart,
You hope with and through My Spirit
You are mine for Eternity.

My Lord let me not fight this enclosing /embracing -
Let me rest in the wonder/warmth of Your Love in total trust.
You have melted me - now mould me if it be Your will.

(After the liturgy, I drove back to Wales, making the following remarks in my journal –)

Left about 12:45 - arrived 21:33 at Llanybydder but have lost my BlackBerry phone - and then found broadband not functioning yet on the new house phone! So, limited contact.

More disappointment but God's Grace overcame - And I noted phone numbers to phone Monday morning! Glory to God for this dispassion. *

*Dispassion is a great gift of the Holy Spirit, when we have surrendered our concerns to God, so when a 'trial' happens that previously would have caused us distress – its more like a wave of the sea that one sees but simply 'rides'.

24th December 2012

Death
Death, hangs around me
Separating me from hope
And love. In Christ I am
Not afraid - but what can I do?
I have more 'stuff' in the car -

Where do I put the books,
Cupboard, screen, tables, boards?
I only have His strength
And in this despair
I have no confidence.
My God why have you abandoned me?

(In the small red journal, I wrote that I went to see my sister, brother and his wife, and my son and family from 24th to 25th down in S. Wales – but came back on 26th December.

27th December 2012

Back at 3 Fisherman's Rest by 12 midday yesterday and by God's grace got furniture moved around to make space for what had been brought from the island.

Had H for a meal last night - Holy Father, have mercy on us through Jesus Christ, Your Son. Forgive them they know not what they do.

**By the light of Christ, in the Holy Spirit - you will be found - upheld, delivered.*

Upheld to bless, deliverer, heal, honour the broken hearted – in Scotland.

Upheld to speak My Word in faith and love - gently, sparingly (ie to set free) , lovingly - in Spirit and in Truth.

You will be upheld because you do not allow yourself to be distracted from My Will - even when in waking despair –(forgive your mother child for her abandonment of you.)

Gently, sparingly,
The Holy Spirit
Comes to hearten
This broken life.

Lifts the eyes
To hope beyond
The clutter and
Despair of abandonment.

All manner of things
Will be well -
And by his grace
Order will be restored -

In my heart
And in this place
That every act
Be a prayer of reparation-
That every breath
Of praise gives life
And hope according
To God's promises -

And so I am lifted
And those for whom
I pray are revisioned
By our unity in Christ.

Glory to God our Father
Who turns all
Things to good for the sake
Of those who love Him.

My eyes are lifted
My hope restored
My love renewed
My grace enabled.
By the renewal of my mind
In You my God.

Protestant

Child - the Prophets spoke My displeasure at the behaviour of those who were called to live for righteousness and love. You have been given great grace to face inordinate degradation to give you confidence in Me and to speak out against the lies of satan that have entered the church.
Man is intransigent without confidence in Me to uphold and lead him into all truth / my fullness that "through Me they may be saved".

A broken life is before You, my God. Have mercy on this broken mind that has sought to hold my life together in the face of intransigence. Beloved, who died on the cross - come into my heart afresh and bring order, right transigence and love - where there has been no love.

The Suffering Servant

Through the curtain
Unknown, unseen
Waiting, hoping,
Loving, the unseen arms,
The calling to greater things -
More faith, more love,
More hope, more trust
In the living, upholding God
Despite the loss, the dross,
The darkness. Trusting
The light of His truth
Even unto death.
And I will praise
You my God
Even in this death
On a Cross.

6

Overcoming Intransigence:

Honouring the Journey of Salvation in Christ

28th December 2012

Unrisen

A broken heart
Lay hidden
Unable to give herself
To the day.
Yet by your grace
She was raised
And in Your Presence
Knew her broken heart
Was with You on the cross.

Bound hand and foot
By the lies of satan
In the church.

Nailed by hatred
Of the Mystery of Love
And the power of Self-giving,
In obedience to God.

O Lord protect me
From all intransigence,
All self-righteousness-
All desire to run away
From this powerlessness
And unutterable sense of loss.

My life in Christ -
Poured out - let no bitterness
Nor shame deny You The Lover
and Redeemer of the World.
Lord my mind is being led
To new territory of humility
And trust in You.

Child, deny not your grace
to overcome,
Deny not your Truth.

"Come to Me all you who are weary and heavy laden - and I will give you rest."

Through the Holy Spirit I weep- yet rejoice at this suggestion that in Christ I may rest and not strive. I was so weary yesterday but trying to create order for Fr Silouan who is coming on Tuesday to bless the house and shed, and it needs to be worthy of You my God.

Child - *in discipline*
in grace
in love - you will overcome.
With Me -by Me -for Me. –

We will create the Noble
Beautiful
and True
all for the glory of God .

One day at a time My precious daughter.

Reflection: If I was 'obedient' to the Orthodox Church (ie the behaviour and shut doors made by men) and the invisible wall, I would have to deny my life in You and deny You.

'Forgive them, they know not what they do'.

Lord I forgive but I know not how to live for You except in the grave or on the cross - forgiving them and suffering. *'Integrity!!'* So be it Lord!

29th December 2013

Waiting

In the night
The barren-ness
Of my heart
Lay exposed.

Empty of love
Of grace
Devoid of truth
Except in death.

But waking
I ask you
To come
And heal.

Come Lord Jesus
Expose the lies
Confess the Truth-
Love overcomes.

My Lord
I cannot,
Will not
Live a lie.

Purify me
My Lord
Break me -
That You are in me.

My daughter, you are ashamed of My nothingness / My humility -
Ashamed of My succumbing to death.
Their lies are nothing in my Kingdom.
But your desire for purity of heart
And love is My delight.
You will overcome all half heartedness

Through grace and truth. Write from your heart .

+

I downloaded the programme made about Sister Wendy who became a nun at 17 and never had any human love or attachment in her heart. But now she rises at 12 midnight to pray because the night is when people need the prayer - what love:

She also said that God wanted people to do things from the heart because they loved Him not because they were told to.

I know in this broken heart that was revealed in the night - there is no will at all. It totally depends on either what God tells me - or other people. The only 'will' is in the passions which are no substitute for God's love, Grace and discipline.

I understand now why when writing about 'little chick' *and her broken legs and wings (and heart), 'Frank' (my rational mind) had to invent a life.

(*This was writing I had done about the abuse many years ago- a sort of allegory to describe the separation of mind from the heart because 'Frank' could not bear the pain of the heart.)

I know, my Beloved Lord, You are giving me this time - this emptiness for healing and restoring the woven cord in You.

But, Papa, my holy God - keep me under the shadow of Your wing that I may keep forgiving, keep blessing, keep enlightening the darkness of despair in the world through prayer and praise.

Show me what to pray, my divine Lord.
Holy soul, have mercy on those who have crucified you.
Give them thanks for this divine honour you have been given.

A Broken Heart

Made in God's image
Born to serve and love
Made to bless and uphold
To cherish and set free -
To honour and worship
The Creator of all.

Yet crucified -
A broken heart set free
To live in Christ
In God.
Willing in Him
To crucify the passions
And desires for human love,
And strive again
To live by the Holy Spirit

In unity in love.

From the brokenness *
This is impossible
So I looked to my Father
For hope and truth
To overcome death,
Destruction and division.

Come Lord Jesus
Come Holy Spirit
Deliver me from evil my God

*PS I sensed that I had to love Christ in His powerlessness in me and I spent the day without will - though I did tidy the shed to ready it for painting - but went -without the ability to judge or say no - with H when invited for fish and chips. And totally forgot to discuss icons with him. It was easy to condemn myself - but without the love of God and the love of Christ, it seemed I could will nothing of good or have self-discipline.

(From where I am now, 8 years on, I realise that purity of heart does not judge, and maybe I needed both the fish and chips and companionship—or more to the point – maybe he needed it.)

30th December 2013

Forgiven

I woke at 6:00 am
And for Love arose,
Though initially no love.

But my Lord -
I want to confess
The shame, bitterness
And confusion I feel
About the tangled mess
Of hierarchs and authority
In the church.

I sensed myself crucified
and torn apart.
Unable to be single-minded
For You -
And finding myself
Self-protecting against ethnicity
And wanting to guard
The grace You have given me.
Heavenly Father
Glorious Lord
Holy Spirit - come.

I do not hide my God -
I do not want to keep
Bitterness or hostility,
but in humility, I come to You -
Lord of all - I do not know the way to go.

(I see, in my mind's eye, Jesus walking through and away from those who wanted to kill and stifle him, without saying anything.) So be it, my Lord.

God's Work

Stay here beloved daughter
Do not run from this struggle
This is holy ground on which
You stand and strive.
This is my work, my hope
My glory you seek
In order to live at all.

You will not be drowned
By the water,
Or burned by the fire-
But you will become My witness.
Do justly
Love mercy
And walk humbly
With your God.

Lord I believe,
Help Thou my unbelief.
Lord without Your Spirit
To give me strength and vision
I have no life or love.
To whom can I show mercy
When I am among strangers

In a foreign land?

My will be done)
phone calls)
letters)
forgiveness of wrongs)
gentleness of manner) Amen
and speech)
forbearance)

(I asked about debt and was asking about an iPhone but at that time no response-
later I sensed the words 'false economy '….)

PS. Oh Beloved - How your spirit, carried, purified, and strengthened and ennobled /enabled me. I even made scones -but even when I returned home after church and lunch at H's was blessed with:

a) sleep,

b) taking apart the dress Margaret had given me to make it my size, and

c) rearranging the desk and small chest of drawers upstairs to give me more space at the desk. Glory to God.

31st December 2013

Reluctant to serve

Lord you have given me so much -
You have asked me to write
Yet I do not believe or act.

I still live with the sense
That's nothing I say will make a difference
And no one believes me.

Lord my eyes are on You -
Holy Scripture is my guide
"Let your yes be yes."

I have sought Your heart.
You have given me Your Spirit
Oh dear Lord have mercy on me a sinner.

I cannot do this
But You can.
I give you my body to do your will.

Oh beloved I confess my sins against you.
I will to do your will.

The devil is hating what I am writing -his schemes, the names he calls me *******, ******** - [even the computer refuses to accept my dictation of these vile names] - overcome by love and truth. Jesus is Lord. Strengthen me my Lord in goodness and prayer -and writing, loving and painting. Amen Lord Jesus in your name.

As I wrote the last note 'Ephesus' came into my mind -I looked up the prophetic word for the church at Ephesus (Rev 2:1) And although they were commended for many things –"nevertheless I have somewhat against thee because **thou has left thy first love."**

V5 "*Remember therefore from whence thou art fallen, and repent, and do the 1st works; Or else I will come into thee quickly and will remove My Candlestick out of this of his place except thou repent.* "

Lord have mercy. *

(I needed to re-focus on Christ and let go of the facets of the Church that took my attention.)

First works that I remember:

1) Spending significant time each day with Your word –

(You have recommenced with your poetry spending time listening and repenting but spend more time with my word -Romans, Hebrews, John and the epistles of Peter and John:
Let my word seep into every pore of your body.
(Jesus prompted me -*what else?*)

2) Being obedient to your requests to write -

3) being 'sent' so- the body was obedient to Your Spirit

'and one more thing'

4) '*go throughout the world '-not physically but through Internet* ***and LOVE the broken hearted.*** - I had been called to 'interpret the Gospel' like St Bede.

I am a worm
so impure and un-loving
but in You, for You
I can do all things.

I will to overcome
the death that destroys
And fills with lies
And self-interest.

(Unbidden) – *'I want you to buy an iPhone today for the greater glory of God the Father '.*
(I tested the spirit- "Yes I believe and trust and love the Lord Jesus Christ come in the flesh")

'I want you to teach / show how lives are saved from self destruction and given deliverance from hell.' Oh Lord Your will be done

1st January 2013

Today having had the way prepared to resew the dress M had given me I didn't try it on, after having taken it in. I just sewed it and it's too tight across the arms!

*I have been shown how I might rectify it as I'd made it virtually impossible to unpick it. I am guilty.

I read St Theophan
about the needs of the body
and how the soul identifies itself with bodily needs –

Nourishment
Movement
Senses.
Only speech is solely 'soul '
As it serves.

Oh beloved Lord Jesus -
I bind myself to You beloved
My body to Your body -
Flesh of your flesh my Husband.
Papa remake me to Your praise and glory.
Help me overcome all that is not of You.
Fill me with Your Spirit
That I do not seek the life that comes from coffee.
Have mercy on me my God

Untangle the jangled heap of false gods that stem from the false provision you were given as a child

sort it out –

i.e. without fear -We will sort out --revive -replace - restore in purity and love .

<u>What follows is in answer to the instruction to face up to the effects of the child's experience on body, soul and spirit. Dear Reader ask the Holy Spirit to help you too identify any on-going effects from early traumas you experienced. It was a reminder to me of the inter-relationship of all facets of our being.</u>

Lasting Effects of Early childhood experience

In Utero Experience

-Not wanted
-War time so food inadequate –
and my mother was providing for
two other children and didn't want me.
-Sense impressions- largely fear

Birthed

-I was birthed very quickly –
from the breaking of her waters
(at the cinema) to birth at
the hospital while she was still
relaxed by the film.
-But not wanted as a girl

Physical Nourishment

-Minimal wartime food -
-Was breastfed for a limited time
-Was undernourished

Movement

(Nothing written in journal here –but used to be put outside in the garden – years later remembered the blue sky and green leaves.)

Sense Impressions

We had one picture of me being held by my mother…but no memories

Lasting Effects

In Utero:

(Only in 2019 did I really address the fact that my mother tried to abort me.)
Likely to grab food that's easy – or fear there won't be enough for me in social situations.
Don't like to be 'enclosed' or 'owned'.

Birthed fast

I tend to grab opportunities and act without considering consequences – grabbing for my needs of life- provision etc.

OR – withdraw altogether because I don't want to be a nuisance or 'be in the way'.

Physical Nourishment

Tend/tended to have careless attitudes to my needs re eating-OR when eating used to allow greed and over-eating to fill the emptiness – not trusting in God to 'fill' me.

Movement
-Overlaid with fear re: the abuse –– & difficulty swallowing

Tend to passivity and unwillingness to serve or give my body in effort.

Sense Impressions
Denied all sense impressions for years.

Healing and God's Truth

Birthing:

God gave me life and provided for all my needs.

Nourishment

Provide good, small meals as needful.

Movement

Freedom in Christ- whatever the situation, whether 'free' or crucified.

Prayer and trust and willingness to consider God's way, purpose- and other people's needs – etc.

The fear of taking action is largely overcome through grace and TRUTH of Christ's grace (love) working in me. Glory to God.

Sense Impressions

-by God's prompting and Grace I came back to drawing and painting and colour in order to paint with the Word; and create calendars.

-God's creation always blessing and He is open to bless and provide.
+

Dear Reader, if any of these reflections strike chords with you, open your Heart door, and ask for the healing Presence of the Holy Spirit to bring you Truth and a healing of your broken Heart and will. Come Lord Jesus.

Death

In the dark I call out to you
My Jesus --my hope -my truth
You are the light of the world
In this death is no grace, or life.

In this pain of loss
Is overwhelming oppression
And lovelessness
Binding me to this horror.

Jesus, You were bound hand and foot
To the Cross -in awesome agony
Suffering for our sake,
And I knew You were /are with me.
And I in You calls out to the Father,
My God, My God why
Have you abandoned me?
Into Your hands I commit my spirit.

Father forgive them,
They know not what they do.
Lord may Your grace prevail
Your Father's love overcome this death.
Your Will not mine be done.

Love

My Lord let me love You
In this death and destruction.
What freedom of movement?

I do not go to visit seaside
Or seek to discover mountains
On which to walk or paint.

I am nailed to the cross
Of dereliction in this tiny place,
Seeking Your Face.

I could divert myself -
at what cost? Can I pray
for those so crucified if I run away?

Jesus, You in me, and I in You -
I love and honour You -
awesome glory, in death forgiving.

But without the Father's grace and love,
No life, direction, purpose-
Except to trust in Eternal life.

My body lies broken and bleeding
covered in filth and bodily fluids
neglected and rejected as a vessel for God.

Oh Lord -in this brokenness I have no life –
"*forgive your mother and fathers who neither loved ,*
nurtured, moved nor blessed you with right senses."

Oh Lord for love of You I forgive –
..I don't want my body - or to be alive –
Oh dear God I hear what I am saying –
forgive me Lord. You gave me life –
forgive me Father -forgive me
I see I totally deny human life –
but my Father You are all to me.
Don't abandon me.

(…My mind raced ahead, then was overburdened by the tasks and shoulds and oughts of the day -on the one hand, and lust/ desire for a coffee on the other.)

Thank You Lord for my body - may it be a temple for your Holy Spirit - in Spirit and in Truth.

Please Lord, take my desires for coffee and tea to give me life in this corpse of sense feeling. Have mercy on me. Give me wisdom and love.

2nd January 2013

08:00

Overcoming

Is it all for Love
That stopped the tea making
So I had no will to rise
Then return to rest in Christ in God?

I seek Your face, love, heart
Not mine-
And I wait for communion
With your Body and Blood
Surrendering my bodily desires
For desire for You.

Let me praise, rejoice
And have faith that
You will give me Grace
To get up and resist
The temptation.

Come Holy Spirit.
In my mind it doesn't matter
If I have a cup of tea-
Because You are so much more-
But the church says
I need to fast;

So for love of You-and by the prayers
Of St Seraphim I will accept this today.

Come holy discipline-
Father have mercy on me
Comfort me in this discipline.
Amen

P.S. (**Written 3/1/13 about 2/1/13) Re: Blessing of the cottage.**

Today Father Silouan arrived early (10.10am) to bless the house - But what he prayed and established was a Hermitage - And with it established my life in God-affirming me in the Orthodox church. A woman given to God. The prayers - Blessing of the water and the 'house' were for healing and deliverance and protection.

Then communion, then lunch-and after a rest we were able to talk to seek answers to my questions which I have noted over the last few days. I have noted the outcomes in my red journal.

But when he had gone and I returned, I knew that God had brought healing to my broken heart through the love and dispassion I was blessed with from Father Silouan (And via him from Father Sophrony whose teaching was passed onto me at a number of points). I realise a prayer about being able to trust had been answered. And because of these my yes to God was deeper, purer and more wholehearted. Yes my God yes. Come Lord Jesus.

3rd January 2013

Worship

In spirit and in truth,
All for God.
Purify me Holy Lord
Lift me to glorify
My Father at whatever cost.

You are my strength
Let me stand in It-
You are my hope
Let me walk in It-
You are my joy
Let me radiate You.

Glory to God the Father
Through Christ
In the Holy Spirit.

Holy soul,
Worship is a secret communion
In the depths
Lifting humanity
To the heights.

"Out of the depths I have cried to you
Oh Lord hear my voice" (Psalm 129:1-2)
Jesus my cry is for You to embolden me
But I know You have to
Ennoble beyond my comprehension-
"Even death on the cross".

I was seeking to rationally assess this to see if it is "true" and was rebuked-
"*Child let My Word dwell in you and feed you-and through you, to others. I need open hearts for there to be change/Love in the church.*"
Now study child-in My grace and provision.

Reflection

Although I studied, I was also led 'out' to do the things I had need to do to fulfil other commitments. As I read the following, written at the end of the day, I am aware of the 'flow' of events, particularly in relation to the purchases of treats for the children. I would not think to do things like that. But their efforts in tidying up were an act of Grace and needed a 'reward' that they could appreciate. I was learning about the practicality of God's love.

PS Got letters written, parcel for Chris and family packed - found a wood place to prepare icons via the woodyard- Took things for post; wood place not open this week; Returned baking tray: Prompted to buy treats for the children-Then drove to Mary's where she and the children had already been working. Glory to God. By 3.30 pm we had got through to the floor of the sitting room and swept it and had our treats. Walked the dog with the children then took Mary to H's to pray Vespers.

4th January 2013

Beloved

I trust in You in this apparent
Greyness:
The defeat of the death overwhelming me,
Nothing human that attracts-
No vision of things divine
Except images of your Saints
And You Lord in your humanity.

Beloved-
My Beloved
Saviour of the world-
Have mercy on me.

Beloved
My Beloved
Christ child of Mary
Ennoble and enable me,
My Lord, to serve Your purposes.

I worship You my Lord
Lover of the Father
Beyond Words;
Adored by the angels;
Crucified by man
Resurrected by God.

Come Holy Spirit

Author - Hope
Overcoming intransigence
Staying still in order to live in Christ.
(Lord, my mind fights writing because I'm saying - 'What is the point?' But even that feeling I have to trust in your hands.)

Listen child -

I want/ need/ desire you to write your story in My hands to the greater glory of God- warts and all- that others may know the truth of God's love for women and the reality of forgiveness.
I will give you insight-wisdom and love to create what is beautiful, good, true and gentle.

Oh Lord have mercy- Show me the way. I am overwhelmed by all the writing and unfinished work I have done and virtually nothing but the calendars brought to fruition.

Child-I have given you writing skills: I will make a way in the darkness-
OK Lord-

Q 1 - Who is my audience?

A *Take the titles I have just given you-Hope*
Overcoming intransigence
Staying still in order to live in Christ.

Choose *by My spirit and aim high.*

A *AIM for a book. - Sections of a book. Just take one step at a time.*

Q Lord I have always just written and see what comes out-Like the calendars-I see what You are doing then I know where I'm aiming-

A. Let it be so.

Q. Lord I have two titles of books-
'All that is in the dark will come to the light'
and 'Don't weep for me weep for yourselves'

A So be it- Make each section coherent and complete in its message (Complete in Christ)-that all glorifies God.

So be it my Lord and hope.

Child - I know you need Me. No one is believing you can do this, but with Me, the Eternal Word, all things are possible.
Jesus....
Holy soul, Have courage to begin.....
Yes do your study first.

PS. In the afternoon I spent about an hour in the studio/prayer cell simply sorting out and assessing the needs for gessoing and painting icons.

I had spent more time in working in the morning i.e., writing re: 'Hope' And had realised that You Lord are the hope to which I am called-You are the fullness of vision through the cross. You are the fulfilment of my life. And there on the first page of Aidan Hart's book on icon painting* were the same words. 'You are the new heaven and earth - through You alone, we can truly see' -And in the studio, I had TOTAL peace - Somehow You were bearing all the pain, sin and loss - not simply mine but of all the world that I pray for.

*Aidan Hart, *Techniques of Icon and wall Painting 2011*, Gracewing

5th January 2013

A love song

Elusive and hidden each morning
I seek You amid the sense of loss-
I seek You in my loneliness
I seek You in my prayer-
I seek You in my hopelessness
And in my homelessness-
And without warning
As I recall the gifts of the day past
I know you Present -
And in all my seeking
Knocking and asking.

You alone the Holy One
Leading to the Father's love;
Hope in Grace,
The holy gift
To stand, yet stand
And carry on -
Even in apparent darkness
Beloved, for ever mine
And I yours.

Embracing, Ennobling
Enabling-
Silencing in Holy Love,
Sharing, Carrying,
Embodying Life Eternal
Now-hidden in Christ
In God.

Beloved daughter
Darling of my heart
Sacred gift to the world
Carry My divine spark
To darkened hearts
Carrying my infinite love,
Forgiveness, Hope,
To darkened places.

Lord if You make the path
And PROMISE not to imprison me
I will go-but you know I
Will/can only go
In Your grace and love.

The Cross

This place
A willing sacrifice
Of freedom
For Your Cross Lord.

To descend to hell
To preach the gospel
To the heathen
To uphold the fallen
To ennoble the weak
To purify and cleanse
Willing hearts-
In me, through me
In you Lord.

Knowing that ALL things
Work together for good
For God's purposes-
Not mine or the worlds.

Oh Lord Jesus Christ
Have mercy on us
By Your precious wounds
We are saved.

Purify and heal me
In body, mind and will
That Your will, Life and Love
Dwell in all of me.

Praying

I pray for the broken-hearted

The powerless and weak:
I pray for the afraid,

the hidden and dispirited-
I pray for children hiding in corners

with no place of safety or love,
Come Lord Jesus-Come Holy Spirit
Come love divine to provide –

Your life was crucified daily by their lack of love, mercy, kindness or gentleness.
But you were upheld by My love and Precepts.
Yes child you had to provide for yourself-According to My Word.
Forgive them, they knew not what they do.

--Child - Now do your study and trust your/My needs in God's hands.

Oh my God have mercy on me in my longing for a mother's love.
I forgive her and bless her- Oh My God, Why have you abandoned me?

6th January 2013

Theophany

Beloved - I worship you
Honour you-Hope in You.

Trust Beloved daughter
In My grace, Truth and love
For you and for mankind.
Believe dear one
In My gentleness
Through you and for you.
Go gently and lovingly
In My Name
For the greater glory of God.

So be it to my Lord and God
In Your Name and courage
In gentleness and love.
Amen.

Most of 'Our' Time this morning was spent in reading Maccabees for the course and trying to do it in Christ so I would remember it - haven't had time to be in Him-hence the poem.

Last night Father S phoned and I had the opportunity to talk about the changes and things that had happened since the blessings and establishment of the Hermitage. The blessings - The invitation to deeper healing and relationship through the fire - I trust in You Lord and pray to love you with all my heart. Fr Silouan spoke of the deep-seated:

Fear -	Oh Beloved Have mercy on me-
Darkness. -	Shine your light, hope and healing
Survival heart -	Into these dark places.

I love you and trust You my Lord and my God. Let me honour and worship You in all things.

(I have just had a smell 'memory' ….!)* God forgive.

Reflection

*Through the phone call of Fr Silouan I had opened the door of my will, to deeper healing. This enabled the work of the Holy Spirit to release memories locked in my body and shut away in my mind. I had ceased to be afraid of these- though sometimes needed more prayer to free my heart and mind from fear or bitterness. I remained free to call on the Healing of Christ, through repentance and forgiveness.

7th January 2013

Gentle healer

You oh Lord
My hope and resurrection
You are the resurrection and the life
And I trust in you.
All fear surrendered in faith -
In You overcoming
All survival attitudes

-Goodenough
-It doesn't matter
-I don't matter
-They don't matter
-Facts don't matter

Oh Lord with joy I drink
Your cup of salvation-
Owning the pain and shame
And degradation-
Every moment brought to the Cross
And redeemed through You.

Peace

Holiness
Deep within
Holiness-A crown of thorns
Deep calls to deep
At the sound of Your waterfalls
My God, my God why have you
Abandoned me?
I am Yours my God

Have mercy on me
Your servant.

(from the Father)
Get up my child
You are without stain
In My sight.
Wipe your eyes
And sin not
Your Lord is with you.
Child - I carry you daily
You have no need to fear
You are mine.
Gentle dove, sacrificial lamb.
All for My glory.
Be afraid of no one
But look to Me.
Papa--I'm sorry
Forgive child-Look to Me.
'The head that once was crowned with thorns Is crowned with glory now.'

PS I took this Trust and did two hard tasks - I phoned BT re: the bills - And an email re: no phone yet - Glory to God.
I took the wood into the wood works in Lampeter to be prepared for icon boards. -
I did more reading for the course-Took the dog on a prayer walk at 5 PM. Lord have Mercy - Glory to you.

8th January 2013

Overcoming death

Death and darkness threaten me
Yet the star rises in my heart
And death cannot hold me.

Holiness - Seeking
Knocking - Asking
For Your heart, mind and will

My beloved Lord;
While it seems You hide
In this death.

Chiselling the hardness of heart
With praise and Thanksgiving
Glorifying the cross of Christ.

Giving thanks for this desert
Where no birds sing
I'm giving my all for God.

Holy Cross I worship you
Holy Lord I depend on you
Holy Seed I seek your grace

7

Overcoming Intransigence:

Death on the Cross and Descent into Hell

Dear Reader, I encourage you to open your hearts to this section without fear or doubt. Often, we have been encouraged to deny our pain, never mind our own intransigence; through misguided guides. As we learn to accept our pain, but in and with Christ, we find the mystery of the Father's Heart – not to deny our pain but embrace it, for the saving of souls and for the Glory of God to be revealed. What is not accepted, cannot be redeemed. Be encouraged to find Your Father's Heart.

Lukewarm

Jesus - Jesus - Jesus
Direct me that I am not lukewarm-
Fill me with your Word,
Hope, Truth, Justice.-

Overcome the lies of satan
The lukewarmness of habit,
That You may LIVE through me.

Child do not deny the injustice
Of the cross - But forgive--
Turn to the Father with the lies
Cry out from your pain
My God, my God - Why
Have you abandoned me?

(I sense the hopelessness - powerlessness - of this death- and in me the sense I just have to accept it and die - and just do what I'm told but with no heart, mind or will except to be obedient, like the eldest son in the Parable of the Prodigal Son.)

Overcoming death II

Holy Father
Like the Psalmist I cry to you
'Haven't I done all you asked?'
And yet still I am crucified.

I believe in Your precious Son-
He is my Hope, Joy, Love-
But I have no joy except in faith.
I rest with Him in death -
But in my humanity
I am blind, deaf and without grace
Or truth. Am I really your beloved child?
I believe, help Thou my unbelief.

Yet I will praise You-
Trust you, Hope in you.
Lord with all my heart
I desire Your will, love and truth-
And yet You had no justice on earth -
So why should I?
In this death I have no anger,
Bitterness or resentment-
Just acceptance and powerlessness.
Do I fight?
How? Is the devil tempting me
To ask for justice?

I no longer believe there is justice
For women in any worldly sense.
But Lord I confess our sins
And desire for reform-

Or becoming power hungry
And losing Your Face.
Forgive us - we know not
What we do.

Untitled

In Your name my God - I die.
Father into Your hands
I commit my spirit. I have no fight
No desire, No vision-

I ask You - In Your faithfulness
To give me Grace and truth
To complete what is started.
Take from me what is not mine

And give it to those who gave it me-
And return to me what is mine.

Let me stand in Your heart -
Doing Your will -
To do justly,
Love Mercy,
And walk humbly with You.

I can no longer see any hope
For myself in this life-
But I wait for You -
And I still have Your life,
And You my God are
The giver of life.

Jesus have mercy on me a sinner-
I have nothing more to give -
No!! -I forgive all
Who have crushed,
despised and rejected me.

Your word of praise

I thank you Lord
For a roof over my head-
I thank you Lord
For the people I know
And for friends.
I thank you for
The gifts you have given me
And the grace to use them.
I thank You and praise you
For the financial gifts
You have provided for me
And enabled me to make.

I thank you for this dog
Who is at times the bearer
Of Your love and wisdom.
I thank You for the eyes
You have given which
See Beauty and Your hands.

I thank You for the heart
You have restored
Which weeps even now
At the broken world
And lack of love for You.

9th January 2013

The Accuser

The accuser seeks to drag me
Further to the pit
Because I fell with the cross
And last night was angry
With Beauty who in her exuberance
Scattered her food all over the floor (again)!

I shamed myself and You Lord
In shouting at her and smacking her-
But yet as I forgave her
You forgive me.

You soften hearts
And melt the ice of loss
With prayer, forgiveness and love
Even from the Cross-
Father forgive them
They know not what they do. +

I read a section of the Divine Ladder about stillness and guarding the soul in the body. Beloved, You have told me these things- But now with this agony hanging over me and in me - I keep wanting to run away. But where - or to whom can I go?

You showed me in prayer that I have never been anything but the work and service I have done. I am nothing but those I have related to.
And now with the sense that those I came to serve reject me - I have no life or purpose. Come Holy Spirit of Truth-

Heavenly Father help me, Guide me- Uphold and enfold me that I may love, forebear, bless and pray - Deliver me Lord- Yet with the prayers of St Silouan I will keep my mind in hell and not despair.

Overcoming Bitterness

Jesus - I worship You
The holy one of God-
Anointed and appointed
By God - Washed in baptism
And anointed by the Holy Spirit.
Have mercy on me a sinner.
I lay my pride, these filthy rags
At Your feet.

Let me love and bless
Those who despise and reject,
As You did for love of the Father.
I pray for the broken-hearted
The despised and loveless.
Let me have no expectations
Except love and to be obedient to your Holy Spirit.

Doxology

Let every moment
Be a joy of praise
And Thanksgiving
To a loving, merciful God
Father, Son and Holy Spirit.

Let every loss
Be counted joy
In knowing more
Of Your love and compassion.

Let every trial
Be received in humility
With prayer and thanksgiving
That I need to lean
On Your heart and mind - Even more.

Glory to You
Oh Christ the King
Glory to You
To the glory of God the Father
Through the Holy Spirit. Amen

Beyond the shadows

By Your Light we will see light -
But yet my Beloved
In this death
The only Light is Trust
And Praise, that You will bring me through.
Come light of Christ
Come Holy Spirit.
Where is your Light my Lord?

You are experiencing My Wrath, My death on the cross where no hope for human life was met.

Where all human interaction was fruitless- -formless- Yes -Like hell -Each locked into their own pit/ world/ desires.

Your own fear of being rejected, despised, and spat upon matches the self-centred fears of others who have decided there is no God - And do not want the Holy Spirit except for their own ends.

Your needs are in my hands - Look to the Cross - Forgive, Bless, and pray for all who despise, reject or ignore you- This is your work in Me. This is your healing and hope. It is not for you to know times or seasons- But to proceed and praise God.   Yes-I will give you strength and grace for this.

Crushed

A flower crushed-
Beauty and form denied-
Fragile fronds
Torn asunder.

Life blood and seed
Denied.

Wordless
Heartless
Childless
No form
No grace
No love.

Looking for the star

I look for the star that rose
Out of Hope –
It is stationary
Over this dark cold place.

What is there
To be born from this
Barren womb?
Where no birds sing.

Forgiveness

Lord forgive me
If I have denied
Your gift of words.
Your gift of life

Hope, Joy, Beauty-
I have sought these
On the outside -
Let me receive Your love.

10th January 2013

Offering

Beautiful Saviour
Glorious star of the East
Bringing true light
Out of darkness-

You offer yourself
Moment by moment
To receptive souls-
Lifting heads and hearts
To Eternity
Changing lives.

Prayer: Extend my boundaries Lord that you may be with me...(Jabez prayer)

(100 X Jesus prayers) 'Lord Jesus Christ have mercy on me.' (I found myself naming people in my heart as I prayed.)

I sensed the fullness of God in each person and thing that is named. "The glory of God "-

- and I knew the darkness in me that resists naming what was unknown and without form or love - Yet destroyed the beautiful, good and true - But because this sin is not assumed (named) it cannot be redeemed.
Lord you have promised that all that is in the dark will come to the light and Your Word says that the Holy Spirit created out of the darkness and formless the earth and all that is there-in through You and the will of the Father.

So, my Beloved, I trust You - That Your light and Your Holy Spirit will enter this darkness, hell, and destruction and create all that is beautiful, good and true. The devil is the destroyer and father of lies-You are the Way, the Truth and the Life. Glory to the Third Day Resurrection. You have overcome death. Holy Cross, we worship you.

Untiled II (I believe this was the Holy Spirit speaking to me)

Beloved of God
Bearer of the Word
Truth seeker
Over-coming one-
All manner of things
Will be well,
In and through
Your Saviour and Lord.

Love Him with all your heart.
-I am with you to overcome-

Make waves in the darkness
By Praise and Thanksgiving
Prayer and total commitment
To seeking, knocking and asking
For the Name that overcomes-
Jesus Christ.
Child - I will set you free to name names- My will be done.

(I had always been aware that although in Holy Scripture God tells Adam to name the animals, I have had a terrible difficulty in remembering (or even desiring to do so) the names of things or people. I could say what they do but not name them, or could remember only the first letter of a name. Glory to you Lord (for this insight.). Come Holy Spirit.)

-**Reflection** - Yesterday I sat in a cafe and was reading Proverbs 3. One verse (v 20) struck me about the 'depths ' and 'the cloud'. But it had no meaning to me and I told this to God. But like a light being switched on - I saw the depths were dark places of the soul/heart (of person or nation) - and the 'clouds' were the blindness or hiddenness that darkened life. I was filled with the Presence in my heart - and carried gratitude with me all day - and the promise* embedded in the verse. Indeed, it is being fulfilled this morning. Glory to God.

***The promise was that through understanding, the depths would be broken up, and through this, the clouds would produce fruitful rain watering the ground.**

Later in the day I was reflecting while praying on very strict monastic or church rules which seem devoid of love and compassion. And the Lord gave me the grace to see that if the monks or those seeking faith in a church setting are coming from a very authoritarian regime, for example having lived under communism, then the 'Christianity' they are able to receive is within a 'rule-bound' context.

The following poem builds on this openness to understand and not condemn.

Ethnicity

Isolation
Self-protection; self-righteousness-
Unredeemed grace to survive.
Fearful and safety-seeking.
Lack of faith in God.

Human bondage
Intellectual blocks to change
Enmity to others
Oh dear Lord have mercy on us.

Forgive and bless
The ethnic mind blocks
Which destroy and oppress
My people.

Child-Darling of my heart
The law is necessary for darkened hearts*
And broken lives.
Do not condemn them
But pray blessings
That by My Light, Love and Grace
And Truth will pierce
The lies and hatred,
And bring kindness, love,
Forgiveness and blessing-
Out of obedience.

11th January 2013

Come Lord Jesus

My only offering my Lord
Is my yes to You-
My desire for You
My willingness to open
My heart door afresh
And welcome You deep in.

You overcome my despair -
Hopelessness - selfishness
Indifference to sin
And fear of rejection,
Failing, falling with the cross.
Oh dear Lord come into
My half-heartedness and give me joy.

Looking to you Lord -
Come Holy Spirit,
One God, one Lord
One Spirit-
Overcoming
The flesh.

Contained
In this flesh,
A temple of the
Holy Spirit
Seeking the Father's heart
Through Christ my Lord.
Oneness in Christ-
Acknowledging the Cross
And dereliction -
Seeking obedience
To the nails that pinion

This body -
Accepting the pain and loss
Of restricted movement
And a heart that cries out
For the broken and lost,
Those lost in the darkness of despair
Without shepherds, or ears to hear.

Oh Beloved Lord, Holy Father
Through your Holy Spirit have mercy
On the lost-
Give us a spirit of repentance
That they may live,
And know that You are God.

Afraid

Lord I am afraid
To face dark places*
Such as You revealed
To me yesterday
At the top of the hill.
Afraid to knock on doors
And offer help, kindness:
I'm afraid to give of myself
In the body, or relate to despair.
Is this the invisible wall
That I will not pass?
I love and will pray-
I have compassion
And seek Your help
For them - But I don't have the will
To give it when I don't see
An open door for me to respond to.
Soften my heart Lord
For your purposes.

*An Elderly lady (86 years old whose father was a key landowner in the village) is apparently disliked for her "rudeness" and I saw windows have been broken in the large house she still lives in; one glass window broken and another plastic covered window in the house she lives in alone.

Dylan (a near neighbour) has told the police who has done it but has no proof to give them. It seems he is her only 'friend'.

"Jabez"
Child, you have nothing but pain to call on in your inner reserves as human, neither security nor love. The ground you stand on is firm only in Christ, in faith. Only in praise and thanksgiving will you 'see' a way. Don't despair child.

Forgive me, Lord, for not returning to you- Not trusting- Not walking on the water. - You have promised this awareness of loss will not overwhelm me - I trust in your Word. Come and strengthen me Lord-Your grace is sufficient for my needs in You.

***Child, Listen-**

Holiness becomes you
You are mine-
Though you pass through the waters
They will not come over you
Though you pass through the fire
You will not be burned-
I am with you.

Repentance

-For your lack of love,
Lack of trust in Me
-For the ceiling and division
In your will-
-For the invisible wall
That binds you.
-forgive and bless the oppressor. +

Reflection after trying to make headway with the Course work: I realised my mind had no real will to concentrate on the course reading or on learning 'knowledge' that my heart, and the pain within it in relation to the cross*****, seems to define as 'irrelevant'. I needed God's reminder to trust in Him.

I heard: *"My daughter I do not require you to complete this course, but for Divine Grace's sake I will allow it - and give you what you need. Your soul is pure towards it. Choose a topic that pleases my Spirit of Truth and Love - Harmony with the - Spirit*

In Spirit and in Truth
Love one another as I have loved you.
Men and women I made them
In my image I made them."

12 January 2013 (Walsall)

01:45

Hell on earth

My head bursts
Unable to countenance
The hell of hidden hurt*-
Trying to make sense
Of the inconceivable destruction
Of every dream, security
And hope.
No bridge but the Cross
Between their world and mine.

I cannot and will not condemn
For they know not what they do-
But it seems that God is on their side
So how do I survive?
And yet God upholds me,
Provides for me and enables me
To forbear, love, and bless.
My God my God why
Have you abandoned me?

***Dear Reader**: I love seeing how God was moving things into the Light…. Once we 'assume' (accept) pain, it will be moved by God into full consciousness and thus redeemable, and we can then choose a God-fearing repentance and forgiveness, or self-pity or blaming others. The choice is always ours. But it is so freeing to recognise our sin and choose to go to the Cross with it.

01:55

Forbearance

I look my God to You -
You have already born this loss
You have borne this pain
On the horror and beauty of Your Cross.
And You have overcome
And in faith in You
I stand with You-
And all are forgiven.

So in your Light I will see Light.
In your love I love -
In Your hands, heart, mind, and will
Are new grace with love and vision.

Hidden in Your heart all overcome-
And no pain to bear
For it is forborn
All sorrow and sighing will flee away.
Amen Amen.

PS., Essay thoughts: Icon of Christ's Resurrection- 2 versions:
1) One redeeming Adam alone -
2) One redeeming both Adam and Eve. What is the truth?

14th January 2013

Reflection Humanly, I do not understand why or even how we can claim to be "Christians" and want to love and worship You, and not love each other - But I do know!- because unless I allow You to break me open - I too want to cling to what I know or makes me secure. Oh Lord, may You be my/our security.

15th January 2013

I overslept having turned off the phone thinking that, like the Blackberry, it would ring anyway. It didn't-so woke at 8 AM-the Spirit having been trying to wake me earlier. My Beloved Lord have mercy on me.

My Father

Beloved Father, I am your handmaid.
Be still daughter-
In your heart,
Mind and body.
Be still in your soul-
You are Mine.
Though you pass through the waters
They will not come over you.
Though you pass through the fire
You will not be burned
Trust Me and love Me.

I have your life in My hand.
You are precious in my sight.
Holy and pure. ....

Deep in the silence within......
"*Glory to God in the highest*
And peace to His people on earth".
Life guarded by angels and Saints-
God my security and strength.
No shame
No name
But God alone.
Come Lord Jesus
Come Holy Spirit
Come Lord of all.

Loss and death
Overcome by love
And purity of heart.

"And the gates of hell shall not prevent it." -I suddenly saw that "the gates of hell" are all the blaming, shaming, Self-denying thought processes that divide and prevent us from loving God with all we are, or ourselves and others. Glory to God. *"Go and pray for the Church, I am with you."*

16th January 2013

Praise

Glorious Lord, I lift my heart
From the mire of my sins
My half-heartedness and inertia
And I praise you.

Thank You; You have given me
Another day to seek Your heart,
Mind and will-To love You
And be loved by You.
Thank You for Your word,
Your beloved Son who
Holds me, yet hides,
Binds me to Him -
Yet disappears.
Holy Hope to not go from me.
I have no strength but You.

Imagine My daughter -*
You are mine
*And precious in My sight***
Let Me wash the dross
As you repent
And I paid the price
For lost hope, dreams, love,
And let me heal, uphold.
Provide.
Carry the cross My beloved
With your Beloved -
Despised, rejected, powerless -
My God, my God
Why have You abandoned me?
Father forgive them they know not
What they do.

*'Imagine' here means 'see' or 'believe' or 'trust'.

** the Father wanted me to write..."Though you pass through the waters. etc..." but I didn't want more suffering - but by His Divine Love - I got it anyway- and He upheld me!!

Grief: *(This is not a spirit of sadness -but deep-seated holy grieving from a pure heart.)*

Unwanted from the womb
Despised and rejected
By the world, Yet
by God selected.

Upheld by holy arms
And unseen grace.
Taught by holy heart
Overcoming time and place.

-Child - It is true you have no strength, body- mind and spirit - but Mine. Be gentle - TRUST and get up in My name. Do not be afraid of the darkness/ name calling -All manner of things will be well.

Lord I believe, Help Thou my unbelief.
I pray for the broken-hearted my God-
who need Your mercy, truth and love
Who need Your word in their hearts-
May they hear your Spirit today
And be encouraged and upheld.
Amen.

17th January 2013

Yesterday I flobbed (was half-hearted) in the grief of loss of life and the suffering of the child who lost everything. Despite that I was upheld.

Half-hearted

My beloved
I was so aware of
This part of me,
The will for good
Destroyed - Without faith
In love or God --
As I stayed with the pain
Throughout the day.

Oh Lord have mercy
On us when we
Seek distractions.
But Lord I know
No food, drink or games
Can heal or change
This gaping hole
This pit of destruction.
I have, by Your grace
Served the needs of others
And covered the pain.
But that grace is withdrawn
And I seek Your face
In this apparent disgrace
And I ask for Your love ...To fulfil Your Word.

Hope my darling daughter
Praise and thank Me
For this holy space
Purified and sanctified
By the Cross.
A holy sepulchre of sacrifice
Waiting for resurrection
In the light of Holy Love.

Purity

With a humble, holy heart -
Given to God,
Lowly, unseen, unloved, unbelieved,
Unbelievable, Pure, Unlovable, unwashed,
Despised - Death on the cross -
Oh Jesus---!!!

Trust daughter!

I am with you.
You are Mine beloved child-
Though you pass through the waters
They will not come over you.

Though you pass through the fire
You will not be burned.
Have courage Daughter - Pray and trust
That's all manner of things will be well.

Father -It's the sense of despair and separation from You that is so terrible and with no vision for hope, love, or beauty. - Oh Papa - this is a path I cannot get off because it is true and pure. Let me not blaspheme against You - Let me not curse You or anyone be hurt. -

18th January 2013

(**Reader be Encouraged):** Just read Theophan re: an aspect of the human person, i.e. the Spirit which raises the human dignity above the animal. Spirit gives fear of God, conscience and the longing for God. Evil robs us, robbed me, of that dignity and the hope and fear of God and longing for God.
All that is in the dark will come to the Light - to You Beloved, through Your cross. Amen.

Aware

My longing for You
My God is in itself a joy
And affirmation
That You are God
And Your word is true-
You Lord Jesus
The Holy One of God
Are risen from the dead
And will fulfil Your promises.

I worship You
Honour You
Thank You
Hope in You for today.
Take me Beloved
And lead me in
The Father's will -
To Silian if it be
Your will - despite the snow -
Or just stay here
And prepare the way
For painting and death
On the cross.

By Gods grace I have written all morning, more or less completing "Overcoming intransigence" -I am in awe of what God has done in my life and accomplished through me. But now the third title I was given to write on is "Staying still in order to live in Christ". Staying in this body - despised - raped- ravaged - no orifice not degraded and made less than human - I'm trying to overcome passions that also are less than divine, through wanting to eat to overcome the hunger for purity and God - oh my Beloved, what AGONY You suffered for our sakes.

Discipline - My God forgive them they know not what they do

I must respect this body and soul - But Lord I invite Your Spirit of truth and love. Come Holy Husband and lover of my soul.

Lord I put these questions
And needs in relation to my body
Into your hands -
I accept these trials and burdens,
Father forgive them they know not

What they did, or do.
I pray blessings for all those who abuse,
Despise, reject the human nature of women
Made in Your image –

Those who crush, despise and rape
Your Presence.
Forgive them -And Lord forgive
Us for seeking
Comfort, or love from half hearted men.
Lord forgive them.
Father God I seek Your heart.
Lord Jesus Christ have mercy on me a sinner.
"Wrath of God against your persecutors"
But Lord I fear that they are in me?

Lord I sense this is to do with my creative work which I tend to crush - my body was denied creativity because of denial of womanhood- despised and rejected- no baby welcome therefore no babies: and until Mary (Theotokos) prayed for me I could not consciously honour her or myself or any woman.

Lord have mercy on me a sinner.

19th January 2013

The Wrath of God

Father, forgive them
They know not what they do.
Left abandoned, unhealed
Uncared for -
A gaping hole
Deep within-
Forgiving, yet unforgiven
No hand reaching out -
My God where are You?

I fear that if I reach out
and give myself again-I will die-
Have no one to care for my soul.
Christ Jesus - Come - Lord I cannot rationally
make sense of this terrible sense of division,
loss, misery of sin. Help me my Lord. –
Come Holy Spirit - Body, soul, and spirit.

At the name of Jesus-

At the name of Jesus
All demons must flee -
Lord I repent for turning
To food for comfort.
I forgive those who sullied
My body-
Piercing and wounding
My soul, body and spirit -

Making me less
Than an animal -
Denying me respect, truth
Denying my voice
And Self respect.
Oppressing and overwhelming me
By their lust for power
And desire to oppress me
Because I stood for Truth
And opposed them.

Oh Jesus, You kept silence
And bought the wrath of God -
Bearing the sins of the world
For our sakes.

This death I bore
Bears down on me still
Because of the rejection,
Denial of grace
And maybe my denial of You.
I am out of my depth Lord
And do not know the Way -
Except to face each day
And try to stay close to You.

Child - I am suffering
with and for you -

I am weeping for the church temporal.
I weep for broken lives and unhealed hearts -
This is Truth -
This is a Time (Chairos) of suffering -
To live in vainglory or by false prophets is a lie.
Your suffering as a child prepared you
For death and gave you purity of heart.
You know you have been carried by My grace.
Humility child is to be hidden in Christ in God –
Not knowing anything except Christ crucified -

Powerless except to forgive, love, pray and
Commit your spirit into the hands of the Father.

How do we survive each day my Lord?

> *Compassion for the broken-hearted in prayer -*
> *Humility in ideas -*
> *Perfection in execution to the glory of God.*
> *My grace is sufficient in all your needs.*

Acceptance of death

Lord I haven't truly accepted
This death and dereliction of hopes
From the recent losses. -
I've wanted it to be mended -
Put right - I've wanted
The pain - The original pain
And loss of life, hope, love
To be mended.
Only in You Lord am I able

To accept - it – maybe it won't be in this life.

I accept - in and through You my Lord
Through your Holy Cross-
That this suffering and loss
Has happened.
And I cannot by will
Or effort, change that or
Take the pain away.
You are God -
And You gave free will -
You gave authority to men-
And I colluded * -I am guilty
For not standing in my Truth with FR
In the first place.
Lord have mercy.

(* Re: denial towards the female architect, who at heart I believed God had provided for both her sake and ours, but by my implicit blessing I allowed another to act impatiently against her.)

It's as if I have constantly
Oppressed the beauty, love, purity
In myself - because of that oppression
So long ago. Dear God have mercy
That I crucified You.
Have mercy on me my God.
I am dishonoured
And dishonouring to Your Name.
How do I bear You or love You
In this death and dereliction
And powerlessness?

My God, My God
Why have You abandoned me?
How can I choose You
When I have no heart or love?

*Come Holy Spirit, fill my heart
With the love and fear of God.
Come Holy Spirit fill my mind
With the thoughts and compassion of God.
Come Holy Spirit purify and heal my body
That all my organs are enlivened and
All my movements softened by Your Presence.*

Comfortless - He hung on a Cross –
No one to care or bless
No one to provide -
His Father allowing Him to share
In the suffering of a sinful world.

Oh my God, where are you?
I'm next door in the shed painting -
I'm at the desk writing-
I'm with H helping you set up a website for your work.
I'm downstairs making a cup of tea.
I will be with you in your tax return -
I AM yours, and my daughter, You are mine.
I will enable you to stand and yet stand
To My praise and glory.
No one knows what you have suffered for My sake.

Denial of love

Child - You are full of love,
Patient, kind, gentle -full of grace
And you are denied.
Do not denigrate your Grace
Because others deny you -
Let Me build your gifts
To share that love –

To give that love
In new ways
In purity of heart.
Use your gift with my blessing.
Undo the log-jam
And get started!!

Gentleness overcomes
With long-suffering and perseverance.

21st January 2013

Justice

In my soul I weep
But in faith I hope
And strive in you my God
To stand for the beautiful,
Good and true.
You have said
You will not rest till my salvation
Shines out like a light.

You my Lord are my Justice
My Hope and my Redemption
Body soul and spirit
Bound to Your Grace
Moving in Your Spirit
Hoping in Your love and provision.

Reading St Theophan about the soul - focusing on the worldly comfort, but in the spirit yearning beyond to higher ideals. Oh my God, in the cross I see only forgiveness as an ideal, and no life - no hope – no gentleness or compassion.

Yet, my Beloved, to seek the inspiration of the Spirit and provide the Beautiful, Good and True is to go beyond comfort zones and gentleness. I have to forget my body and weakness and seek Your heart, mind and will. I have no physical, mental or spiritual strength apart from You. Beloved - My God, My God, why have you abandoned me? Jesus, Saviour of my soul - I worship you - Honour you who died for me.

Tears of Witness*

*Prayed the Jesus prayer and 'Hail Mary' instead of Vespers and wept while praying for myself, but also for the world for broken, unhealed hearts in the Church.
I repent Lord, of surrendering
All my gifts -
And I weep at this broken life.
But I sense the tears
Are coming as healing balm
Coming to reveal the striving
Of the child trying to please,
And overcome the pain in the dark.
But here now in Your Light -
I'd choose to stand in Your grace -
Choose to stand in Your love.
Yet without Your divine spark
Of inspiration my Beloved
I can do nothing.

Help me love, give and repent
For the broken world.
I cannot seek beauty
Without gentleness
In my spirit and soul.
Holy Father I worship You -
You allowed, wanted, the Cross
To save mankind -
Leading me in Your truth.

Child born in the dark
Have the courage to overcome
Your own desires, needs and dislikes
*And go the way of the Cross.**
Bookbinding, Accounts
Icon painting and preparation.
Above all - in all
Praying, repenting, forgiving.
- A vessel of Beauty.

* This refers to the deep desires of a 'child' who is constantly tempted to desire the good things of the human life, that create a sense of well being. But God is reminding me that I need to keep looking to the Cross for a greater good. And in fact, it is true- there is no lasting satisfaction in worldly human joys as my desires are conformed to Christ and His obedience to the Father's Purposes.

Hopelessness/Lovelessness
Runs like a cord
Through body and soul
Attaching itself to my spirit -
The lie of satan -the lie of aloneness and abandonment.

Oh Lord, with all my heart I reach out to You my Lord
to hold Your hand in the dark.
I believe, help Thou my unbelief.

Dear Reader:

You see through this Section God's work in bringing pain out of the darkness and helping us make informed choices about our response, rather than merely having a hidden reaction to it.

But we still have old thought patterns to overcome – and so 'Lord I believe, help Thou my unbelief' is crucial to keep putting the burden back on the Lord. WE cannot fulfil our life in His, we can only keep opening the doors of Faith, and obedience to the Holy Spirit. Glory to God.

8

Overcoming Intransigence:

Restoring Life in Christ

Lord I put today's needs for service into your hands - there is a need bursting in me - wanting to proclaim joy, love, greatness in colour but it is tied to a cross of orthodoxy - Holy Mother pray for me - blessed St Seraphim - Help me. Let this desire to stand for You Lord bear some fruit.

22nd January 2013

From Bitterness to Prayer

Beloved You were given bitterness to drink -
You did not deny the taste
But refused to drink it.

Glorious Lord, Risen from the dead,
Holy, holy, holy art Thou oh Lord -
I worship You; I honour You undivided Trinity.

Father, I worship You -
Call on you, hunger for You-
Receive my prayer for Your people.

May they be united in love,
Gentleness, purity of heart,
Humility and grace.

Forgive them Lord,
They know not what they do
Have mercy on them.

Help us Lord to let go
Of what we've had and been
To live in newness of life in faith.

Many churches are in turmoil at the present - I pray particularly for those seeking to buy and move to new churches on mission for Christ. May Your will be done.

Let me heal your broken heart -
Let me put balm in your soul
Let me provide for your needs today daughter -
Let me do it child.

"FORT KNOX" **-Can only be opened through prayer, thanksgiving, gentleness and love.*

Child you are having difficulties with icons because you do not believe you are 'real' and the devil's lies are still alive deep within. Yes I know My dear one that you look to Me to lift you -

Shall we do it?

* Fort Knox is what the Spirit has called the hidden strongholds of pain in the unconscious, but which affect aspects of my life.

"All that is in the dark will come to the Light."

Despised
Abandoned
Rejected
Worthless

The TRUTH - Lord You were never worthless
even on the Cross or in the grave –
whatever situation You were in –

But many women feel worthless because of attitudes in the world and in the church and their experiences of being silenced, oppressed, or simply denied or ignored, quite apart from overt abuse and violence.

I suppose deep within I accept I am worthless.

No daughter - 'A precious jewel in My Kingdom'

I praise You and thank You for my life
I praise You and thank You for my spiritual death and resurrection
I praise You and thank You for all the trials of my life
And the grace You gave me to overcome
I love You Father, Son and Holy Spirit -May I do and live Your Will and You come and live in me.

"*Child- The vertical element (of the Cross) is larger - NEVER forget that in your relationship to God the Father and incarnated in Christ.*

Your Strength

If I do not guide you My child - Your works are 'dead' –
And come from your unhealed soul
- led by unmet needs or bodily desires."
In the Orthodox Church –
Their culture has overtaken their faith...
Do not despair.

My God, my God why have you forsaken me?
My soul is in anguish because You made me female - a woman - And my Love is denied - My hope is gone. Oh my God have mercy on me - Father forgive them they know not what they do. I praise You, I love You.
Father forgive them, they know not what they do - Forgive me for abandoning hope in You.

Guilt?

They are not guilty
Your grace condemns you. (i.e., Because I choose to forgive, as Christ did, I am bearing their sin.)
Grace to bear their sin,
Grace to forgive.

The Love of God the Father has allowed this -
Yes- "the sacrificial lamb". (It seemed St Seraphim was speaking this to me through the Holy Spirit.)

Your will be done my God.
'*Re: coffee: there is still a child wanting comfort, alongside the dying to self needed to write, work at book binding or painting. Be patient and forbearing of your needs.*

Lord forgive - I am not surrendering to Your Grace -
Lord I trust, help Thou my lack of trust.
'As the eyes of a servant looks to his master,
as the eyes of a handmaid to her Mistress,
So our eyes look to You, oh Lord.'*

Although this comes from the Orthodox Vespers Service, it has become part of my own prayer life to the Lord when I seek His direction for my life.

23rd January 2013

Beloved of God

Glory of the Father
Beyond comprehension
Given to God at birth,
Proclaiming Jesus Son of God
At eighteen;
Upheld and providing -
Provided for and blessing -

A child of God...
Broken and bleeding -
Returning to the sheepfold -
Held in God's hands
A servant of God
In immortality -
A broken and contrite heart. +

I was woken this morning with the thought of addiction, and: every morning to get myself up I make a cup of tea and take my vitamins. I am grateful to God for His mercy - But I felt this morning that this is a sin - separated from trust in God to provide for all my need.

Lord I turn to you - I don't hide with this but maybe this is my thorn in the flesh? Maybe this is your comfort for me 'in the flesh', when there is no one but You in the spirit. Lord have mercy.

- Gentle soul, allow me to indulge you, as a husband would. You do My will all day - trust re: addiction - Let the Father work this out. All surrendered - All standing in the light. Amen.

Let us get up as instructed to write - And be ready for the post -God willing-.

Papa - I cling to you in my insecurity - Wanting always to do Your will, in Your way. (Oh Papa - Why have you abandoned me? I heard a cry from the heart for my mother - Lord have mercy.)

24th January 2013

Have mercy on me a sinner.
To you alone be glory.
Forgive me for desiring to be loved
Blessed and forgiven -
When I am so full of myself
And my own desires?
Blessed Lord have mercy on me -
Show me my pride -my sin
O glorious Lord -
But I lean on you –

I have no hope but You-
Father, Son and Holy Spirit.
I have to go and pick up these tyres
Today - Give me grace to complete
The sewing of the book, and glue the cover if possible -
Oh Lord have mercy on me -
I fall with the cross.
Let Your Name be my hope and strength.
Lord Jesus Christ have mercy on me.

Boxed In

I am boxed in by sin
Which I cannot fight
Except by blaming others
And accusing men
Through the centuries-
Of hating and despising
And rejecting women
And calling it tradition.

So holy tradition accuses me –
Of wanting, needing, desiring
To **live** in the church for Christ.
Oh Father have mercy on me -
Purify and heal this broken heart
And wilful mind.
Your will be done.
I seek not power but Love.

Lord Jesus Christ, son of God
Have mercy on me a sinner;
Condemned to death?

25th January 2013

Glory to God for the grace of yesterday - Father Luke had sent the book cloth and many more gifts for bookbinding but they only arrived yesterday, rather than Wednesday, with the practical instructions on how to do the sewing.

H emailed to say we could go and get tyres so I had till 11.30 to start sewing the sections of the book together - all but five done.
Went to Strata Florida after buying new tyres. An old Cistercian abbey - A stronghold of 'Welshness' (as witnessed by the signs and 'information' boards around the ruins) - Yet Lord they served you and prayed to You.

Jesus I will never understand nationalism from your perspective. Forgive them Lord. They know not what they do

Pride of man - strong walls.

The Flower: Glory of God

- Love given and received

Littleness - The Flower

The flower is what it is:
It is hidden in the heart of God -
Dependent on Love to bring it
Into the fullness of being.

It does not design itself
Or have pride in its beauty.
It flowers whether it is seen
By human eyes, or not.
But it glorifies its Maker.

Painting glorifies Me
My darling daughter -
From ages to ages.
All creation tells of My glory.
Man that made walls of hate,
Fear, self despising - allow
Death and destruction.
Will you allow Me to ask you to paint - today?
Your will be done my God. What do you desire?
I don't want you to concern yourself
with details of what and how.
I will fulfil all that - if you say Yes.
I say 'Yes' my God but You know the book has to be completed
today so it can dry -
And you know that they don't really need it if H is at church!
OK Lord. Your will be done.

(2022 Comment – How often my clinging to a task with "false gods of need" have stopped God's blessings! I have been brought to see that any facet of 'self-importance' which does not align with a real provision of service, is a false-god. Service is a real reason for doing something; but so many times I or others cling to actions because of habit, pride, or indifference to what God is asking of us.)

Man

Made in the image of God -
Given the power to name
And have authority over creation -
Leaning on, empowered by
God the Father and creator of all.

Holy, Holy, Holy Lord Jesus Christ
Redeemer, Purifier, All wise,
Surrendering to the Cross
To pay for our wilfulness,
Disobedience and vainglory.

But through You the world
Is brought back to the Father,
Through You we can glorify
Our Creator and Redeemer
And look only to You to praise.
Amen, Amen, Amen.

Child - Your childhood was so devoid of holy love - No you cannot see what is still hidden - You were carried by God - purified and healed so you could be His servant and bearer of His love . Yet deep within was only loss and death - always seeking to pull you into the mire and depths. ***Love, Praise and Thanksgiving*** *IS My saving grace. Joy and peace come through Me and doing my will - loving and praising and trusting in all things. I will unite all men and women when they desire My Kingdom - My Lordship in their lives. Yes daughter, child of God - Let down your barriers and let the flower have space to bloom!*

The Flower II

Unseen
Unheard
Unloved
A flower moved
Within the seed
And the seed
Found love
In which to grow -
And gave itself –

To death
That it might
Break open
And grow
And provide
The world
With a flower,
And more seeds
Of love and beauty.

Embraced

In the arms of love
The seed hopes
And trusts in the Eternal
To water and fill with Grace
This earthenware vessel
Which yet holds within it
The lies of darkness
Seeking to kill and destroy
The holy seeds of love.

Lord have mercy.
Deliver me from evil
And give me obedience
To Your Holy Spirit of Truth,
Love, Mercy and Hope.

Lord I believe, help Thou my unbelief -
I sense my walls Lord –
And the wonder of Your promise within.

Child - Your life here in this place is not as in Craigmillar – (when I was living and serving in an impoverished area of Edinburgh in an old person's flat.*)*

Overcoming inwardly is as important a journey as the outward overcoming and serving of Craigmillar. Both death - but this is an inward and upward purification that your soul may be saved - totally surrendered to the Cross - according to your prayer to Me - And My Promise to you.

'Justice is mine' says the Lord. Oh Papa - So be it. Your will be done.

26th January 2013

Fruitfulness

Looking to my Father,
Listening to my Lord
Embracing the Holy Spirit
Standing in Love,
Gentleness, Purity and Grace.

Surrender to the Cross
At every moment –

Looking to Love Divine
To bear every event,
Act, word in His love.
Taking every attack
As gift, and praising God
For His love
And repenting - Oh my God
Have mercy on me a sinner.

Falling with the Cross?

Gentleness - Holiness
Crucified for our sake
Oh my Beloved Word
Love Divine
Have mercy on me.
I disregard You
I ignore You
And didn't get up
When You woke me
As I'd asked.

I will to be obedient
To Your Holy Spirit
To Love Divine.
I don't want to lean
On earthly comfort
When You have given me
Rest the night through.
O Delight of my heart
Have mercy on me.

(I have omitted a long reflection on a computer scrabble game, when the level was 'hard' and the computer used words, I did not know, and failed to accept some words of mine that I knew were legitimate. I reflected that we could not share boundaries...and no two people share the same experience and boundaries ...so how do we communicate? - only in God's love do 'all things work together for good.')

I cannot search in my mind for meaning - But I can look to God and ask. Like the other day when I knew I did not grasp Proverbs 3:20 about the depths - I looked to God - And He turned the Light on - and suddenly I 'saw' the meaning - I understood and was comforted by the Promise of the coming of understanding, and rain from the clouds that had obscured. new life.

Lord, are You teaching me that when we become like a seed in Your Kingdom, hidden in Your Heart - we grow through your Holy Spirit as we turn to You - in Purity of Heart, in Love and desire for understanding. Like a flower - waiting to bloom until the plant has grown, firmly rooted with leaves – and through You we have union and understanding with others.

*Thomas, Take one step at a time - in My heart - With My hand and My obedience to the Father's purposes.** My bride must be purified and honoured in her sorrow - and lifted to glory.*

(** After the final abuse by my step-father and the 'death' of will and hope, my mind tried to 'make a life' through the intellect and to protect the heart. This is usual for many abused and traumatised children, and adults. I became good at finding and keeping the rules, but all 'comfort' was thrown away. Here it seems that my mind is owning its inability to 'save' the heart and soul but God is already providing….) The following is a form of affirmation of the childhood experience, by God, which my rational mind had tried to deny and ignore, but God was tying my life to His Love.

Trampled on, suffocated, despised and rejected.
Unseen, unheard and despised.
Daughter of the King.

Oh my Father, why have you abandoned me? I don't understand the church - Why don't they believe in You - why are they not obedient to Your Word and love and bless their enemies? Why don't they do what they tell others to do?

Child - They do believe but they do not have the same boundaries as you.
Papa - I am so nothing and You so everything. How can I live save in Your Love?

Be watered with My Love My daughter -
Sacrificial lamb be comforted by your place in My Kingdom.

(Thomas – i.e., my mind) Oh my God - I cannot comfort this child - this woman –

No, Thomas you cannot comfort this grief and sorrow - But you can rejoice in your repentance and sorrow for her sins in running away from her loss and childbearing capacity.

Come Holy Spirit - unite this broken life and heart - to the praise and glory of God.   Body, soul and spirit, I surrender all.

Go in My Name child - You are Mine.

27Th January 2013

Gentleness

Oh my Beloved, Darling of my life -
Your Light redeems as it breaks open
The hardened, darkened places;
Bitter and insecure,
Unwilling to reach out in love
And gentleness,

Hope child, and do not let
The sight of unredeemed darkness
Turn you from Me or from
Trust in the Father.
You are redeemed by the Cross.

I will not despair my Lord
In such little trust and hope,
At this unredeemed will.
I kneel before You - all given -
All broken dreams and hopes
Laid before You in tattered shreds
All good is Your work, not mine.

Hope blessed of God -
Trust in the divine promise
Of grace to overcome
Of love to carry you
Of vision for each day
And purity of heart
Through your holy Mother.

In my nothingness
I worship you -
May all that is within me
Honour, praise and glorify
Your holy name -
Jesus Christ, the holy one of God.

Gentle child, blessed of God -
Chosen before all time.
The agony of the Cross
Is for all time
A Mercy of God
To bring salvation
To all men,
And to bring all
To the knowledge Of God.
It is not for the faint hearted
But for lovers of souls,
For those that hunger for God -
For Love, and repent of their sins,
Maladies and self-interest.

Hope child
For Grace, trust and vision
For each day - Sacre Coeur de Dieu.   (*Sacred Heart of God)*

28th January 2013

Justice: Love and Mercy

Love and Mercy shine
In the darkness of sin,
Corruption, and injustice,
Overcoming division,
Self-interest and desire for power.

Like twin lamps guiding
The Way, they cannot
Be darkened or quenched
When they result in
Forgiveness, forbearance
And the Truth of the Cross.

This is justice -
To receive and live
The work of the Cross -
To accept dark places
And in His strength
Shine in Grace and Love.

This is to "do justly,
Love Mercy, and
Walk humbly with God.*"

Glorious Risen Lord, Alleluia.
Your grace is sufficient
For all my needs.
(*Micah 6:8). +

Lord - I have to acknowledge that self interest rules in me too-

Oh dear God, have mercy. Let me be obedient to your Spirit and continue the writing on the computer without allowing the pull to game-playing to divert me. Show me how love and mercy are fulfilled in righteousness and truth in **You.**

You have suffered daughter all your life from domination of those who provided any form of love, attention or provision. I want to set you free in Me - Free to bless, pray for and deliver your enemies, who know not what they do - enemies without and enemies within like comfort eating.

(I had prayed for understanding - Thank you Lord - Fill me with your grace, Truth and love - Heal and use my broken heart for your purposes. I know you heal for service in Love - Amen Lord, Amen)

29th January 2013

Yesterday I discovered I had to do my tax return, after having previously arranged with Fr Silouan that I would opt out. I asked St Silouan, Fr Silouan and St Seraphim for prayers. I was carried through the day till it was finally completed at about 5 PM and as a result have £45 back tax coming to me-DV*- and could bless Chris. (*DV is Deus Volunte – God willing which is a way of acknowledging we can presume nothing, but in humility pray and hope.)

Glory to God - Chris and the children went to church on Sunday. May they grow in love, oh Lord, in You.

Child - Now go and write further sections of what I have asked. You are Mine - and I yours.

Father God - I lean on you -
Blessed Saviour I open my heart
To Your saving grace;
Holy Spirit come, bring Your Truth
To darkened places.

Thank you Lord- for my life,
Every trial, every overcoming -
Every joy, every loss,
Every blessing, every curse -
That you are God and carry me,
Enable me and encourage me
For each new day.

Lord the 'to do' pile
Includes all the work of the course,
And all the work on the icons
And the writing on the computer
And liturgical prayer.
I have little heart for the reading
But when I do it You give me blessing
In your Word!
Oh Papa, Have mercy on my soul.
Have courage beloved
To let go -
Put the day into My Hands
And trust Me to provide
For your needs.
In all things, darling of My heart,
I will provide.
Oh Papa - I long to come home to You but I will praise You, trust you –
And rejoice that You are God -
And You made me, formed me
And love me. Oh may I glorify you my God.
Forgive me when I forget Your image,
Or forget You my beloved Saviour -Deliver me from evil.

Child I know this seems unrelenting pain -The agony of the Cross is real - the isolation -the cut-off-ness from life and people and purpose. Have courage child to persevere in faith, hope and, above all, love. You are Mine, and I am with you. I will NEVER forsake you.

+

My God help me accept what happened - has happened -I believe it's for a greater good - I pray for all the abused - despised - raped women, children and men. Lord have mercy.

30Th January 2013

Disfigured

My Lord on the Cross
You were disfigured.
Beaten, bleeding, unlovable -
Dirty, despised,
But Your Soul still forgiving.
Your Heart breaking
For the lack of Love,
But You forgave.

I no longer know
The way my God -
Except to call on Your Name -
You seem to have abandoned me -
And yet You call me to the Cross -
Bleeding and dying.

My heart is broken and hopeless
I seek to hold on to Hope in You
My God - even aware
That all I am is of You.

What more do I release Lord
In this place of dereliction?
Oh my God have mercy
On me. I forgive-
Please forgive me. +

Revealed: As I sat and stayed with the feelings of this poem, I sensed the buried ANGER- always suppressed for fear of retribution - always buried and emerging as pain and sense of loss. Truly God was bringing the darkness to Light, and with it the sense that it was 'their fault' because I had never had control over what was done to me.

"I want you to admit My Name into your anger - Allow us to purge your guilt and unmet need to be heard and understood."
Jesus?

Allowing the anger expression - The following prose poem is my first attempt at allowing the anger out, at expressing it. …

Ranting at God

My God why did you make me a woman who suffers? I am powerless against You - Because You are God - And powerless against men who think they are so superior and God-given even when they are often wrong, in context or misguided in understanding. And women have to agree or simply end up being confused, oppressed, and stifled out of fear - Or seeking to be obedient to Your apparent will. I know that Your Spirit unifies. Does the giving have to be so one-sided? Unity in what?

Re: Do you not want to call the lost to you and feed them? - -Oh my God , my God, why have you abandoned me? Why my God did you bring me into the church?

I'm sorry I didn't just apply for a council flat and go and serve in Edinburgh and keep quiet... It all comes back to my powerlessness to change anything in this world except myself and I've tried to conform to serve needs - I thought for Your Sake.

Oh my God where are you?

My life is a Cross. I cannot see or believe in the church - But my Beloved that's not strictly true –

Jesus come to me - Holy Spirit of Truth come to me - I cannot shut You out. Help me - Purify me.

Hatred of being a woman - Of your vulnerability, lack of freedom - because of your fear of abuse.

Anger - because when you moved in My Name and My Purposes you had no fear because you trusted the Father to protect - But now the Father has not protected -and you are abandoned and subject to worldly temptations and sin as you were as a child.

Oh Heavenly Father, Forgive me for hating being a woman. Forgive me for my anger at my powerlessness and the behaviour of men. I repent. But I am without hope - Oh Lord forgive me for my arrogance. Jesus hoped/s in Your promises. I hope, help Thou my lack of hope.

Your Word is life – Oh God have mercy on me.

There's a door in my heart - bolted and barred - Come Lord Jesus. (In that moment I was praying and listening….)
My God why have you abandoned me? Hatred of my Self - My purity, loveliness, desire for God - which resulted in this death.

I open the heart door to let Jesus in - But only the Spirit is there - Life itself.

Child: Be disciplined
Be holy
in My Name - You have no strength apart from Me.
Be loving
Be gentle.

The Hell of the Cross

All the agony of separation
From the Father's love,
All division of the bitterness
And selfishness of mankind
All received in Your Body,
Your soul and Your mind -
Oh Jesus what hell.
Yet You came to save.

So I pray for souls in hell
I pray for broken hearts
Who need courage to face
Salvation, repentance
And forgiveness for the unforgivable.
Lord only You can do this.

Weep not for me but weep for yourselves.

Lord we live in denial
To be able to survive -
But we do not truly live
Have mercy on our souls.

After Matins

Relentless suffering - For my sake -
Redeeming souls from hell
Sacrificing your life, for My Life -
Suffering because you see
Those who are meant to love, bless, serve and save,
Caught up in systems, relationships
Which serve themselves and not those
Who cry out for Good Shepherds.

Powerless to act on the cross of dereliction
You despair - Yet remain faithful
To prayer passed down through the centuries
Despite the living prayer you have in your heart.
Have mercy Lord - I don't know Your Will accept your word says to be obedient to authority.
Let Me live child –
In willingness to love and bless
-In willingness to pray for the Father's mercy -
In gentleness of heart and voice.

Amen Lord - But I feel raped and there is a defensive spirit waiting to pounce on anything that wants to bury me in a church with mixed messages.
Lord I am willing to be willing to do Your Will if you show me.

Child - All of this agony has to go on My Cross each time you suffer for My sake –
You will suffer but hand it on for My sake that you may live, as well as die, for My sake.

P.S. By God's grace, I read Judith and Esther in the Masoretic text and did some icon work. Glory to God.

31st January 2013

Resurrection

Lord God - I hold before you
The icon painting and the mystery of love
This embodies - The learning and doing
The praying and embodying,
Lord have mercy.

You are God- I trust.

Pro plasma technique

To begin with -
Gently starting from the dark
And creating the light.

Oh my Beloved- I hope in You
And your Grace - Your hand
Your love.

Thomas does not believe
That this is work for You.
But I pray Lord - You will teach me
And fill me with prayer and love.

Thomas you are not forgotten -
Listen to My heart and write for Me -
Paint for Me My daughter -
All one in Christ in God.
Love and forgive.
Serve and provide in ways
They cannot to do for themselves,
In stillness and rest -
Gently in prayer and love.
The Father: *Paint my kingdom daughter*
To my praise and glory.

1st February 2013 (My 70th birthday!)

Born Again

Born in the flesh - Despised and rejected
Born again in the Spirit
And all the heavens rejoice!
Oh my beloved Lord.
I believe, help Thou my unbelief.
Darling of My Heart
Have courage to stand
Love, bless, uphold in My Name.
Lord don't let me be a hypocrite -
Living for You is easy –
But full of temptations to sin
And to despair – So hard work
To maintain purity of spirit.
And I fail in my will for good.

To whom shall I go?
You have the Words of Eternal life.

Oh Lord let me rest in you -
Though I do not ask for rest
But to glorify God the Father.
....
Deep within, lovelessness
Lies lurking, brought to light
By Grace -
No root of love - Except in God -
No human resources to call on -
But I call on you my God and King.
Heavenly Father have mercy
On the unloved. Can the dead praise you?

Have mercy on the broken-hearted -
The unhealed hearts throughout the church.
May they find your grace to live
And glorify the Father.
Your word is my hope
My God - Your Presence in faith
My strength.

I cannot work this out
Or think a happiness.
I trust you to carry me through this day
I pray for unwanted girl babies - unwanted women –
Have mercy Lord.

P.S. Lord forgive me - I suffered the Cross all day - Praying - And accepting M's talk - Dear God -Your will be done, but let me see/know/live it.

(M came with an individual 'cake' and some pasta from Sainsbury's to wish me Happy Birthday. She sat till I finished some gilding - quite hard for anyone, as breathing is not welcomed when gilding with gold leaf!!! So we then went into the cottage and had a coffee and talked. What grace she was given, to come to bless me. Glory to God.)

2nd February 2013

Gentleness

Come holy spirit - Deliver me
From all indifference to sin.
Burn in me all the rottenness
Of past hurts, that clings like
Drifting seaweed and hide the truth.

May Your love dear Lord
Strengthen and Purify
My Heart that I may be obedient
To your Word to let your Light shine.

You Lord are my light
You are the Lampstand
Because in You alone I stand.
Authority in the church
Crushes my spirit Lord
Because I am a woman -
Do I crush You too?
Do I allow all the lies of satan
To overcome me and deny Your/My true life?

Come Holy Spirit of truth.
Beloved I need you - I seek your face.

....

Shush darling one-
I am with you -
Be still and know
That I am God.
Justice is Mine says the Lord.
Child - I want you to understand - Lovelessness - What you were living through yesterday - Leaves you powerless to bless or act - This is the nature of the cross. Go in My Name today and get what you need.

Lord I do not understand the unity of the church, except in terms of us all looking to You to lead and provide in Your Word and Sacraments and by your Spirit in our hearts and lives ever seeking to 'save souls' from eternal damnation.

They seem to say the unity is in the Bishop. But do the bishops have interest in women as your servants? with Your Gifting? So we have to be obedient to the structure of services... But how do I deal with my love and concern for the souls of young /all women and the oppression of their souls by false gods?

How do I relate this to my desire/need (?) to paint icons and all that entails of learning from those more deeply embedded in this work of glorification?

Lord, please make it clear - what I must do -I beg you Lord Jesus -

Gentleness beloved -
Seek, knock, ask -
This weekend -
Pray at all times
And love your neighbour
As yourself

Go In My Name and Spirit
Be forewarned of spiritual trials
And do not succumb to despair-
You are not without Grace or Truth
You are Mine.

3rd February 2013

Sacrifice of Praise

I am caught between the leaven of the Pharisees,
(Desiring to be obedient to authority

in the Orthodox church)
And the humility of Christ obedient to the Father -
And in loving Him, accepting crucifixion.

God's mercy upholds me
In tender mercies,
But the cross of dereliction
And the powerlessness to act
Pinions me.

My God and Lord - Yet I will praise you-
Yet I desire you-Yet I seek your face,
Heart, mind and Will.

May Your will be done in my life-
That I live for you-
Come Holy Spirit of truth
Deliver me, and guide me
In your Beauty.

Father forgive them
they know not what they do.
Lord I choose to live - for You.

Child – I am giving you a new Heart –
And Spirit – a new name
Forever more.
Get ready to go in My Name and Love.
I AM with you.
Do not despair child – You are Precious in MY sight.

9

Overcoming Intransigence:

I prepare a Way for you in the presence of Enemies

4th February 2013

Provocation

Come Holy Spirit of Truth, Love and faithfulness-
Overcoming the cold (and over-high electric bills)
I refuse to allow the comfortlessness
Of this cottage
To rob me of the Peace of my Lord
And His trust in the Father to provide.

Rebuke of God:
Child- Obedience to grace
To paint icons – and meanwhile
To draw them and get to know them
In prayer, praise and thanksgiving-
Is My provision for a broken soul.

Lord, my mind seeks to please You and wants to provide for the broken-hearted, the lost and unrepentant. Have mercy my God. But I have terrible darkness as I sensed this morning – such despair and wanting to run away and destroy myself.

I surrender my intellect and memory to Your redeeming power my Lord Jesus.
Have mercy on me.

Your will be done my God.

As I provide, prompt and ask – day by day, moment by moment – be patient, kind and strong to save – in prayer and blessing. Do not be afraid. All manner of things will be well.

You are conformed to the Cross
Father forgive them, they know not what they do/did.

5th February 2013

Out of the Darkness

After descending into hell
The Light of Christ brings love
And union.
Truly, at the Name of Jesus
Every knee shall bow

Love alone has Strength
And Power, Love alone
Has rights – in Patience,
Forbearance, Gentleness
And Love. Glory to God.

No fear hidden in Christ
In God – no waves
Or anxiety can change
His Peace or Trust
In the Father's Promises. Amen, Amen.

Gentleness

GO in My Name and My Grace
In all things – Practice My Presence
And do not be afraid
You are NOT alone or abandoned…

6th February 2013

Waiting

My Beloved is waiting
But I am afraid:
My Beloved is hoping –
And I wait for Him to lead me
Prepare me,
For His Love to fill me
In His Plenitude.

And I am hidden-
Hiding in the shadows
Of God's wing-
Seeking the courage
To step out to Him.
Come Lord Jesus-
Come Holy Spirit,
Prepare Your bride
For Love. Amen

P.S. I was overwhelmed with GRACE and accomplished many tasks re: icon board preparation and preparing for a small shed which was being delivered.

7th February 2013

I was 'awake' in the Spirit before dawn and realised I was praying that I would know what was after this year. Where am I going? It was the Holy Spirit or my Lord that was praying. Amen Lord Amen.

I stopped going forward with the application for the 3 year Icon Painting Diploma, because I sensed I was to rely on the Holy Spirit....And since I made that decision it is as if my grace has been restored! Glory to God. Come Lord Jesus.

Holy soul, let Me complete My work. Let Me fulfil your mission on earth.
Let Me write your story in art – in hope – in Truth in Love and in words.
I want you to live without fear.
Do not be afraid – You are Mine –
Though you pass through the waters–
They will not come over you;
Though you pass through the fire,
You will not be burned –
You are precious in My sight – and holy –
A precious, precious jewel in My Crown.

Writing for the Cross –
Holy in My Sight
Precious Jewel
Willing to Serve.
Be still and know that I AM God.
It is I who have made you.
In My image I made you-
Deformed (for righteousness sake) by the Cross
Forgiving and holy-
Holiness in Heaven and on earth...
Do not judge yourself daughter
Be at peace –
One God – One Lord – One Spirit-
One Truth. ***Love alone is Pure.***

Willingness to serve man and animal must never over-ride My Purposes for your life. Be PURE in intent – I will provide for their needs.

I want you – (darling daughter) to be still in Me never moving from my Presence. Have faith I will provide for all your needs.
Title for Study: 'Don't weep for Me, weep for yourselves.'

P.S. Re: Shed… In the end the promised help couldn't come and with the help of angels – I put up the shed with no other human help….and got the extra wood I had bought cut into shelves and put in place in the cottage.

July 2022

As I write up these pages, I see how God was preparing me, yet know there were more trials, but He would be with me, and I was precious to Him - even as He was beginning to lead me forward.

I understand these words now, around 10 years ago. but I never fail to be in awe of His desire, and need, for us to love and serve His purposes through the work of the Holy Spirit.... How much need we have to be purified and sanctified. Like the Iceberg that only has 10% showing above the surface.... how much have we in the dark that we need to give God permission to bring to the Light?

It really is about a growing surrender, and yielding to His salvific work, including taking up our cross to serve according to God's purposes and leading. I am including one more series of poems within this time frame which brought more pain and loss to the surface. As I listened to what was being revealed in my heart, crying out my pain and sense of loss, it is as if the darkness stands in the Light of His Truth and Wisdom -And it melts away!! .... The poems show once more how the Light of His Spirit and Word led to my unity with His Spirit. Then directions and instructions about what was coming next can come to Light. And God waits for us to 'GO' in the Light of the New integration of the redeemed facet of the soul.

Share this journey with me as we move onward, being prepared for the next stage of the journey.

8th February 2013

Peace to His People on Earth

I love you daughter-
I desire you to know My Name.
I am with you now
And for always.-
Though you pass through the waters
They will not come over you;
Though you pass through the fire
You will not be burned.
Call on My Name -
Surrender your soul to My Care -
Oh my God...!
Do not be afraid.

Deliver me Lord from all unrighteousness.

Hope in My Name

Lord forgive me for my self- protection,
Self-giving, self-organising…
To You alone be all glory –
I trust in You
And Your Divine Truth.
I love You Jesus
The Saviour of the World
Come Holy Spirit
Drive this darkness
And all spirits of defeat –
False desire away
From Your Presence
And this Temple for You.

12th February 2013

Glory to God

Overcoming half-heartedness
Means facing my own sin
And apathy and lack of trust in God –
Without faith that God will provide
I cannot stand in grace.

So glory to God in the Highest
And peace to His people on earth.
I surrender ALL of my mind
Into Your hands my God
Though crucified – yet glorified –
So I will trust in YOU my God
The Holy One crucified by hatred;

Glorified in death-
What mystery –
Father forgive them
They know not what they do:

- Commitment for today:
- 2 faces in preparation for the icon
- Reading for and starting the work for March Seminar paper
- Possibly preparing for gilding.

Precious lamb of God,
Join Me in Praising the Father,
In a hymn of Praise, Love and Thanksgiving-
Your death an offering Pure.

Go in My Name.
- I went and served.

13th February 2013

Deliver me my God from all
Lust for power, praise, or well-being:
Let me serve and love even in poverty of spirit,
Trusting in Your Divine Grace to persevere
And overcome.*
In my half-heartedness, have mercy on me.

(P.S. I sensed death – yet the Holy Spirit worked through me – letters to the Monastery nuns – calendars printed and posted, and prayers offered.)

(*This prayer probably stems from the Prayer of St Ephraim which is said during Lent – but re-presented from my heart.)

Overcoming Death

Jesus, my Hope and Joy;
Jesus my Life and Defence.
Jesus the Light of my eyes;
Jesus my gentleness.
Jesus, my death and resurrection;
Father forgive them
They know not what they do.

I sense the death of girl babies;
I live the dereliction of forced marriages –
Of rape and sexual subjugation.
I fear the oppression
Of senseless men –
And I see You Lord on the Cross –
Bearing our pain – paying the price
For their sins and mine.

Beloved souls – you weep for Me –
When you weep for them –
Innocence destroyed, Beauty deformed;
Compassion-less self-interest
bringing death to souls or bodies.

Deep within rebellion cries out Lord –
Father forgive them – but I cannot willingly
Submit to their yoke.
Help me my God -I believe, help Thou my unbelief.
Oh my God, Have mercy on their souls.

Icon painting? – *Without love it is nothing.*
Child – do not strive to be acceptable to Me –
Do not be concerned about what others will say-
I will provide for your need and your desire for purity.

A child in the dark
Alone.
Helpless, hopeless
Unheard, unhealed.
Human loss
Covered by Divine Grace.
Weeping, homeless;
Loveless
Family-less-

Still-hoping in God
To provide –
If she perseveres
In good works
And loving others.

But my Lord, as You bring me healing, I ask for Your protection from self-harming – from the cares of the world taking me over, or running away from the cares of the world through games or art.

Show me, guide me, bless me Lord to persevere in Love and Faith. Father, Son and Holy Spirit, may I love You with all I am, according to Your Word.

Clinging to the Cross

I am at a loss-
Aware of the enormity of Christ's gift
On the Cross –
Aware of how I have been carried
With little human care or parenting;
And carried now
With the loss of the island monastery.
But Lord in knowledge of my isolation,
It's hard to trust that
You will provide!
I no longer know
What to look for –
Or how to love and trust.

Lord I trust You,
Help me with my lack of trust.

Let me surrender all vain hope
And let me hear Your voice
And see Your Way.

I love You Jesus-
I love You Holy Father –
I love You Holy Spirit.
Please uphold me in Your will.

Hardened Heart

I see not feel how beautiful You are.
I am in this desolate place
In the cottage, and in my heart.
I do not want this pain and loss-
I do not praise You for this cross –
And dear Lord I cannot escape.
Heavenly Father show me the Way.
I have tried to be good enough,
But where are You in this silence?
Have faith
Oh my God have mercy on me-
Don't let my feet or tongue slip
From Your pathway – I will to praise
But I feel terrible – no consolation-
Only death of hope, love and purity.

I cannot 'work this out'-
I repent of all arrogance
And separation from this suffering –
Along with millions of women and children.
Suffering the cross in innocence.
Please help me my God –
I sense I am losing the desire to live.

Jesus crucified – the Way of the Cross –
'Your will not mine be done'.
I say 'Your will not mine be done'.
But I do not know Your will
Except to get up and work on the icons
And go and see the house.

Lord I am guilty of despondency-
Yet I will praise You.

OWNING THE LOSS Following the poem, prayer and allowing the powerlessness to 'have its way' – I lay down again and prayed within – staying with the pain in my heart. There were body memories re my mouth being forced open, and a sense of choking, but following this, deliverance and tears.*

(Healing *I am in awe of the immediate sense of release, comfort and integration I experience when something like this is brought to the Light, and the shame and isolation of the soul at that time is removed – not simply that Christ brings healing through the Holy Spirit, but that my Inner-Being becomes more integrated – literally the broken heart becomes more and more Whole and I am not denying my own needs or suffering. Truly I am loving and honouring myself in new ways.)

I was carried through the day.

Oh dear God thank you for Your mercy – tidying and cleaning downstairs; getting the shed prepared for gilding – and making the decision to send for a lighter gold.

19th February 2013

Trust

I praise You and Trust You
My Lord, to enable me
This day.

Darling of My Heart
Light of My Eyes
We honour you.

Glory to You.

Lord I put into Your hands
The car – its needs –
And my need for a vehicle-
And desire to have one
That costs less to run.
Your will be done.

Child- BELIEVE –
You have given yourself for My Purposes –
Be confident My dearest daughter
That you will be provided for.
You look to Me – and Love-
Be My Leven in the World.

Do your painting with My Blessing –
In prayer, praise and thanksgiving.

13:34

At Matins, as I prayed for 'those in authority and hence prayed for currently debated, 'redefinition of marriage bill' and abortion – I found myself praying for (not only those aborted) but for those whose mother had tried to abort them - I sobbed and sobbed. Beloved Lord have mercy on this life-less soul who cannot live – and even if You give life – then it gets aborted.

This is why the recent loss is so painful – I thought You had given me life in You – but You show me that there was no pure life without loving unity. Oh God have mercy on our souls.
21st February 2013

Broken but Not Defeated

A broken heart sees all the
Degradation of the soul,
And the lies of satan
That seek to entrap me
In defeat and loss.

But You Lord break through;
And somehow grace
Makes a way and Your Will
Pierces. Dear Lord have mercy on me
And may Your Spirit prevail.

I do not know how to continue
In this darkness and despair
Except to praise and honour You
For carrying and upholding me.
But Lord, guide me in Hope and Trust.

In Your Redeeming Love, Grace and Truth,
I hope and trust – through me,
And in me. Oh death where is your sting?
Or grave your victory?
The Cross alone has victory.

Sacrifice your 'Hope' for 'Joy'.
'The tender mercies of our God.'
Gentleness in all things-
Let My Spirit enfold you in My Love,
You are Mine, and I AM yours.

Do not strive but rest in My Presence.
Trust My darling daughter.

HS- *Marina – your will is broken-*
Do not strive, forgive them,
Look to the Cross
Blessed are the merciful
For they shall obtain mercy.

Oh Jesus, You had no strength on the Cross –
All power taken from You – all grace given.
I surrender all my Beloved to Your Love.
I Love You my Saviour. I love and honour You.

P.S. – I sought to live in praise all Thursday (21st) and on Friday He made it real as joy in my heart see entry below.

23rd February 2013

Yesterday (Friday) I woke and my prayer was answered;
The Holy Spirit livened my soul to perseverance
And commitment to His work –
St Theophan reinforced what God was doing –
And I had joy in my heart.

P.S…I was sickening with a cough/cold which got worse on Sunday and led to me resting on the bed most of Monday.

But in the sickness and 'defeat' God showed me the broken and confused human heart resulting from the abuse. Totally incapable of making 'sense' of the violence, and literally 'crushing' defeat of my body. I could not decide, will or act. And that is what I was like. (My sister said I went through a 'depression' at this time…but maybe this is the spiritual nature of depression – when the world you knew and 'acted' in and related to, has been destroyed.)

…but the Lord showed me through a game, I could choose again – and will to do good and overcome defeat. Glory to God.
Your will be done my God – I love You Father.

1st March 2013

Adoring

Beloved I seek You
Praise You, adore You-
Pierced Head, Hands,
Feet, Side – for my sake,
Our sake, for all the world.
Such LOVE outpouring,
Such mercy forgiving,
Such gentleness given.
Oh my Jesus Come.

Dear Bride of Christ
Come to My Arms-
Every moment to My Embrace.
Let your loneliness melt
In Our Oneness-
Let your weakness disperse
In My Grace –
And let your pain and loss
Rejoice in My Embrace.

(I found myself wanting to ask about the future and 'Where' I was going to find a place to 'be'- to put a shed for painting – and I weep – 'Oh my Beloved forgive me for not trusting You to provide. Give me the courage to trust a) Your courage in me to overcome, and b) the provision of the Father.

You have always provided – forgive me Lord.
TRUST my darling daughter – I will never leave you or forsake you.

God is Love
Your will be done my Lord.

Go to Edinburgh – knock, seek, and ask for accommodation from July onwards…*
Go…Ask, Seek and Knock. You are in My Hands, Heart and Will. I will provide.

*This was a confirmation of two different people asking me to go to Edinburgh. One was an invitation to an 80th birthday party, and the other a phone call from Father John, my Spiritual Father, the senior priest from Edinburgh. – But also showed me where I was going next.

2nd March 2013

06:30

I hide, my Beloved under the shelter of Your wing –
I bury myself under the covering of Your Mercy,
And am carried into the Day of Your loveliness.
Blessing fruitfulness in the Beauty of Your Gracefulness.
I exchange my tiredness for Your Life,
My weakness, for Your Strength,
And I praise You, Father, Son and Holy Spirit God
That You are my Delight, and I am Yours.

Reflection

I did go to Edinburgh and was so grateful I did despite the challenges of being with people again.

This was the last time I would see Father John alive, he was in bed most of the time by then and very weak in the body, but still able to be alert to the Spirit's promptings….like phoning to ask me when I was going to see him. I thank God for that love.

I stayed with M and during that week in Edinburgh I frequently 'fell' with the cross…but the Lord reminded me:

Child- be patient, praise and give thanks.
Have courage for today.
Go in My Name.
You are Mine.

This is indeed our Truth. But how often we have to fall to learn – 'In all things be thankful.'

Came back via Manchester (Friday night) and then Walsall on Saturday for the course; and got back to Lanybydder on Saturday for 10.30 pm.

I was blessed with a visitor to the cottage for two nights, and her leaving on Wednesday left exposed a 'hole' gaping in my heart – the pain of a child needing love, protection, gentleness and the 'covering' of a parent. But You Lord upheld me and provided for what needed doing in the world. Amen and Amen.

Despair

Emptied – alone – abandoned-
No grace it seems to overcome-
YET I WILL PRAISE YOU.
YET I WILL TRUST YOU.
YET I WILL CONSPIRE TO DO YOUR WILL.

Dearest Lord I abandon You
And refuse to listen to You-
Deep in the pain, loss and despair
Of death and dereliction –
The filth and blood and pain –
The emptiness and powerlessness
Of death waiting to engulf me.

But in You I trust in Your Word –
Your Way – and I believe Your Love
And overcoming through Your Resurrection Power.

I will give myself to You to write,
As You gave Your Spirit to me –
To sort out the car insurance yesterday.
Your will be done.
I love You Lord Jesus, Darling of my heart.

Gentle Soul – Listen to MY Will at every moment-
Listen to My Heart beating in the Love of the Father –
Wait for My Spirit to embrace you in grace
And Love My darling daughter.

P.S. – I went on to write over 1,000 words of the re-vamped essay!! Glory to God.

16th March 2013

Darkness…..

How do I bless and love
Give and receive
Tied to a Cross?
How do I honour
And glorify You my God?

Listening

Solo – yet united
Sovereign – yet subject
Single yet united to all,
Delightful, yet severe –
Gentle but always firm.
All for God.
All for Love.

I will make a way in the desert –
Delight in the Garden –
Spend time with Me.
Delight in Me.
Rejoice in Me.
Be 'bent' only to Me.
The Father will provide.

Why be downcast oh my soul?
Yet I will praise You my God……….

Oh dear Lord may I grow in grace
To Stand and yet Stand
And praise Your Holy Name –
You have promised that
Those who sow in tears
Will come home reaping and rejoicing.
So Lord I pray for all the broken hearted
Who seek Your Face and Life
And 'demand'* help in the
Name of Jesus Christ.

*I had difficulty writing 'demand' as I don't believe I have any right to demand anything – barely to 'ask' for anything – I simply have to accept what 'God' gives, good or bad.

Reflection 2022 – I want to re-enforce here for all readers who have suffered abuse and live with this same lie. God did NOT WANT or plan your abuse. But it happened – and God will turn it for GOOD if you allow Him. Listen to what the Spirit spoke to me after the above.

Marina Carrier

The broken hearted embraced by God -
Who heals the broken-hearted -
Delivers from evil
-overcomes the darkness and
Brings all that is in
The dark – to the Light.

Lord I praise You and thank You for my mouth –
I will not deny what happened but thank You for bringing me through and bringing all to the Light to Your greater Glory.

Enlightenment

When men degrade the body – the soul is traumatised and degraded. It cannot respond freely to the Work of God and hence the division of soul/ body and Spirit.

The will for Good/ God is broken.

The Hole

Like an explosion blowing an open chasm –
So my mind and soul were blown apart
And devastation reigned –
Broken bits blown into mindlessness
With no apparent hope of repair.

And now, facing this chasm and loss
Only Your Cross puts salve on the wound
Of my heart – and for the millions of savaged children
Whose soul, spirit and body have been unhinged by rape,
And unspeakable violations, Lord have mercy.

Jesus, come, bind up Your broken-hearted children,
Living as half-hearted men and women,
That they may be Whole Hearted for You
Bearing Your Image, Mind, and Will in Love,
Counting every loss acknowledged as gain in YOU.

TRAUMA

I am reading more of 'Memory and Abuse: Remembering and Healing the Wounds of Trauma' by Charles Whitfield.

'When there is no healthy environment to discharge traumatic memory (which I learned recently gets locked in the body rather than the mind MC) – it remains repressed.

'The human unconsciousness is a place or repository where we store cognitive information and emotional energy that relates to our past traumatic experiences that we have not consciously processed and healed to completion, and about which we are not fully aware. (p.99).

He describes the 'psychological behaviours connected with this state as:
Dissociation: mental process of disconnecting from ones thoughts, feelings, memories or sense of identity.

Repression: - suppressing /crushing/squashing feelings, needs, desires/thoughts so it remains unconscious.

And **Denial:** it didn't happen – that isn't important', etc.

I am aware of how these continue, but also of the courage and grace, I am given to turn more readily to Christ in prayer, praise and trust, to own and feel the rising emotions and memories, rather than use avoidance of them. The poetry over the last 4 months has enabled this more and more and I know 'my Redeemer lives'.

My Beloved, I confess my sin of turning to games, to fill the sense of emptiness and lie of 'no one to turn to' – I forgive, my Lord- Please help me.

FEAR
FORCE
SILENCED
HELD-DOWN
NOTHINGNESS
BLACKNESS
STRUGGLE
STILLNESS
DROWNING
LOSS
DEATH
EMPTINESS

Forgive him My beloved daughter- and all those who have taken from you and given nothing – those who have counted you as worthless because you were female; or denied your life on the cross.

Lord I forgive – but give me patience to wait for Your Life in Love.

REFLECTION…

Over the next few days – other memories came to the light, sodomy with shame, and the emptiness of my heart because of my mother's inability to want me despite my illegitimacy!

But God was also clarifying and purifying my thoughts and false self-blaming.

27th March 2013

Hearted

Beloved child of God,
Your tears are Holy and Pure-
Your Love is gracious and true-
Your prayers are God Honouring –

And yet you suffer without need.
Stand My dear one in My Name-
Stand and fight in Love
The lies of satan and pride of men –
Bless them and purify them
Without strife or anger-
They know not what they do.

I will give you words to say
I will put a new heart in you.
I will provide for every need.

(I see that in standing in Christ…I don't need to suffer personally – as all I have is compassion and prayer! Hurrah for God.)

Praying about the Church and fear of being a cause of disunity, then the Spirit inspired me:

Unity

Child- you cannot ***cause*** *disunity through Love and Truth.*
You may shine a light on that which exists.
You may bring into the Light the darkness of the work of the devil,
and you will be blamed for disrupting false peace-
But stand firm in My Holy Name.
You are a witness to LOVE.
Others have to choose the Cross for themselves – choose Me – or
lies/ deceit/ vainglory

29th March 2013

Daughter of the King…..you choose My Narrow Way even in your dereliction of soul. Have courage to open your heart door to self-sacrifice..

I'm not asking you to overcome but to give your pain and loss – to own it – to believe it – to trust in MY Purposes for it. Let the world know the human heart without denial.

Worthless?

I look at this dereliction
of my soul – my worthlessness
as a woman in the church –
The truth and love I hold
Counted as nothing
By men who hold the reins,
The temporal power to build,
Or cast down.

But He who Truly has the Power
Listens, knows and sees
And He prays within me,
'Father forgive them,
They know not what they do.'

And I wait in the Arms of Love
For the Father to uphold and bless me,
To provide for me in this world,
And the Next, through Christ my Lord.

New Life in Death

Death falls on me like a shroud,
Their intransigence making communication
Impossible, like speaking into a fog.
And it embraces me, blinds me,
Yet quickens me in Truth.

What mystery of Love
Brings Hope and Strange Vision
In this place?
Why do my eyes light up
In Love beyond seeing?
In Faith beyond knowing?
In Unity beyond their intransigence?

Father forgive them
They know not what they do.

And Silence is my communication,
Hope and Love is our Unity-
Silence is my answer to their lies.

2nd April 2013

Under Your Wing

I hide under the shadow of Your wing
My God – forgive me for my tears
And self-pitying weakness and fear.
Let me rejoice in You – surrendering
To Your grace, Truth, Love Life
And Hope in God the Father.

I stand against the lie that I have no future
In You- I have Eternity and in You I have hope.

Beloved may I look and see through
Your eyes of mercy, forgiveness, purity of heart.
Have mercy on me my God, Have mercy.

Forgive them.
They are without comprehension
Of the gravity of their sin-
And separation from the Beautiful, Good and True!

Yes- women sin against themselves
-colluding with men's intransigence.

Trust gentle daughter
That your tears will water hardened hearts
And soften the ground to prepare the way
For healing, purification and the glory of God.
Child do not despair at your weariness
And fatigue in the struggle to overcome.
By My Spirit praise, trust and LOVE.

I will Lord to be always ready for You to prompt me to write/pray for the needy. I confess I am sometimes 'busy' and don't respond to Your prompting. Let me be willing to write to the Plan children, & to Joy and Pam. Meanwhile I pray for them and trust in Your goodness.

Child- Your willingness to serve is My Joy. Trust in MY Providential Care, and My grace to overcome ALL darkness.

I AM leading you through the Valley of the Shadow of Death. Have courage in My Right Arm.

Reflection

This 'new work' becomes clearer with specific teaching about '*gentleness as a state of being*' having no resistance to the Presence of God, nor the flow of God's energies….all focussed on loving and serving the Living God….
Later: '*Meekness is a gift of God*' but it must be received.

On **6th April** I noted the grace I have been blessed with to make 'blog' posts on the new website – then to add an email address to the website….but the Lord corrected my naming of it and called it 'A Word for Today'.

He also commented: *The further descent into hell is necessary for a greater rising.*
Darling of My heart, Your Light cannot shine when it is hidden in darkness.

8th April 2013

Silence in Death: Seeing Resurrection

Death embraces what was
Resurrection Embraces what is-
His Hope, Purity, Vision
Providing, enabling, envisioning
A life of trust, faith and Truth
In a Living and Loving God
Through the Holy Spirit.

A life of Joy, Prayer and humility
Seeking the approval of no-one
Yet loving everyone.
God is Love.

Awesome Glory, I worship You
My Lord and My God.

The Word

Hope in the Lord
And do good.
Hope in the Lord
And serve.
Hope in the Lord
*And purify Your heart**
Hope in the Lord
And Love.
Amen

('Trust' – may all that is within you glorify God. All intentions for His glory.*

18th April 2013

I have an entry in honour of **Father John Maitland Moir**, the priest who brought me and blessed me, into the Orthodox church. He had recognised God's hand on my life (in giving me a prayer life like a 'monk') even though I was still a RC when I was first obedient in going to see Fr John in Edinburgh. He died on Wednesday 16th April 2013, after a time in hospital. Father Raphael had warned me on Tuesday he was failing, and I wept. But when Helen emailed, and Katherine phoned me today to say he had gone from this life on Wednesday morning, I wept again. He gave me such an example of love, never judging, always seeking to provide both spiritually and materially for his spiritual children. And always respected me in Christ, even when I was suffering.

I went up to Edinburgh for the funeral. I discovered S was to go for respite care as she is not coping with different carers coming in to see to her needs. On a subsequent visit at the beginning of June, those currently looking to her welfare pointed to one particular care home for her as the social worker decided she was not able to go back to the house. We visited it and chose her a room. The social worker and others arranged for the move on June 7th. The current Power of Attorney asked me at some point if I would live in her house if I came back to Edinburgh, to be there to oversee the renewal of the house.

It was agreed that I would move back at the end of June.

But meanwhile, I had completed an icon course with Aidan in Shropshire in May, and then in June went to the Monastery. The Nun gave a talk based on Elder Paisios's teaching….we must surrender ALL things to God. – things work out without our intervention….

without obedience there is no healing; without healing no Love.
In a crowd, keep your peace by praying for everyone. Elder Paisios also said we needed to 'dig deep' in ourselves, so all illusion, pride and malice and insecurity is brought to the Light so we find the only true security in The Rock – Christ.

Whilst at the Monastery I met Fr J's wife, who gave me a

'counselling' session…hearing what had been going on in opening up to the pain. She suggested I let, 'the little girl write the truth. It seems to me the only Truth I have is the reality of the things that were done to me, and God's Truth in forgiveness and blessing of my enemy, and grace to overcome!! Truly he knew not what he did…in terms of his right-mind.
I wrote a Haiku while there:

Loving grace o'ercomes,
Beauty shining in darkness-
Moonlight making day.

Reflection The Sisters were given a second talk while I was there…and as I read it now I realise I was being provided for in relation to what was coming. It was an encouragement to not enter into 'stories' or long explanations with others; but be patient with those that do. Chase all approaching provocation by turning to Christ, and prayer, so instead of being a burden to others with anger – we can carry His joy and help lighten the load of others.

And maybe the Lord enabled me to remember these wise words, and all He had taught me in Llanybydder, for the first poem I wrote having taken up initial life in S's house in Edinburgh to prepare a way to move there:

Oh my Beloved,
I sense You crucified
In this lovelessness -
Other people making
My boundaries
And taking my life
As they did Yours.

And yet You forgave
And You call me
To forgive, forbear
To bless and save
Through prayer
Service, and
Blessing.

Oh Holy One of God
Come to my darkened
Lonely heart and
Hearten me with Love.

Come Lord Jesus-
You alone
Comfort me and redeem me
And enable me to serve
As I have promised.
I rejoice in You.

P.S. **DEAR READER:**

I have often thought that our Spiritual Journey through Life, is a little like one of those video adventure games. As we journey, we meet different characters, trials, enemies, and have opportunities to pick up 'spiritual gifts' which we then need to choose to use in a subsequent 'trials' in order to keep moving forwards. But always we are journeying and moving onwards to a greater and Eternal goal.

On this leg of my journey I was blessed beyond words with two fundamental gifts:

1. the certainty that God the Father, is Love and provides Life and Hope and Purpose for those who choose Him, so I do not need to be afraid of what happens; and

2. 'the strengthening of my inner being, that Christ may dwell in my heart by faith (Ephesians 3:14 -19) is a promise fulfilled as I seek His Word and obedience to the Father.

Instead of running away from the pain within, being overwhelmed by it, or ignoring it, I was blessed with the opportunity to listen and surrender to the work of the Holy Spirit bringing the dark to the Light of Christ. Christ suffered with me and now in this redeeming work, He IS my Inner Strength and the Truth.

You have completed reading the book, and hopefully you have been encouraged to seek, knock and ask for yourself in your Life and Faith. I truly believe that if you give yourself and God – even 10 minutes 'listening-time' a day- God will continue to build, heal, purify and clarify your life in Christ. Step by step He will lead you to greater redemption and integration of the hidden, and the lies and defeat attached to it will find the Truth of the Cross. You will gain His Grace and Love, alive in You, hidden in God, and become a Light bearer.

Good Strength and courage dear soul to make the Jabez Prayer, your own: **Lord bless me! Extend my boundaries, that You may be with me, and I may cause no hurt to anyone, or myself**. (I Chronicles 4:9-10)

P.P.S.

You might be interested in the **2nd Book of the Trilogy** "He Heals the Broken-Hearted"

"Your will be Done: Beyond Powerlessness and Fear – Revelation of Life in Love".

If you send me (marinax7@btinternet.com) an email with the book title as the subject, I'll add you to the mailing list for details when it comes out.

Maybe we will meet in person one day- either in time, face to face, or in the Heavenly Realms? Who knows? Till then Au-revoir. God Bless you.

Index of Poems

E

F

G

H

U

W

Y

Printed in Great Britain
by Amazon

35643632R00169